The Po

True Crim...
Arcata,

Arcata, California is a special place, where
redwoods meet the sea, where frisky university students,
staunch traditionalists, ardent world savers and
dedicated leisure specialists mingle on the town square
and where the weekly newspaper documents it all
with unconventional enthusiasm.

From The Police Log:

• January 5, 1996 3:14 a.m.
Nighttime on the square, so enchanting
Till a man filled the air with loud ranting
Police hushed his tone
And he walked home alone
With the spirits he had been decanting.

• February 19, 1996 10:25 a.m.
With "scruffy" beard, denim coat and pants
He strode up G Street, looking askance
At campaign signs there on display
And tore down two along the way
Then scampered, sans apology
No theme of ideology
Defined the scruffian's design
A witness said, "He was out of his mind."
On the Plaza, post-conniption
Cops stopped a soul of his description
Who fast denied the dirty tricks
Disclaiming hands-on politics.

• August 4, 1998 8:16 p.m.
On Valley East, trouble arose
And evil's dark face was exposed
When thieves, hearts gone hard
Went into a yard
And ripped off a guy's garden hose.

• June 29, 2000 5:88 p.m.
Imagine the creep-out factor:
A resident of the 1600 block of 11th Street went out to her car
and found the door opened and the inside rummaged through.
What scaly, wraithlike hands had passed over her stuff?

• **June 15, 2000 11:26 p.m.** Some guy's writhing face-hole erupted with halitosis-borne verbiage that made up in volume for what it lacked in decency at Ninth and H streets. A brush with adult beverages preceded the event.

• **September 8, 2000 3:13 p.m.** Stark sunlight warmed the exposed nape of a traveler, slumped chin-to-chest in classic alk-stupe mode in the back of an APD cruiser on the way to the Pink House via the alley behind Tavern Row.

• **January 15, 2001 12:22 a.m.** Possession of marijuana, possession of alcohol, possession of a driving-impairing liquor buzz. These are the things that make Arcata Police officers grow a big ol' frown. Being from Visalia is somewhat excusable.

• **February 18, 2001 7:45 p.m.** "Could ya, like, kick down a couple of coins and help us out, myaaan?" beseeched the feeb at the ATM in a full-blown marijuana accent. The cannabinoid cadger had shuffled randomly off in a macro-scale demonstration of Brownian Motion when police arrived.

• **March 30, 2001 Late report** A traveler's Bic-flickin', cig-suckin' nic-fit on the Plaza ended with a cop-greetin', code-quotin' cite-signin', butt-grindin' denouement.

Kevin L. Hoover is the editor of the Arcata Eye, "America's most popular obscure small-town newspaper," and writer of The Police Log. For 10 years, at three newspapers, he has documented errant doings in his town's streets and neighborhoods to the delight of readers, the amazement of colleagues and the exasperation of journalism professors. This book is the first compilation of his work.

The Police Log

True Crime & More from Arcata, California

By Kevin L. Hoover
The Arcata Eye
2004

The Police Log
True Crime & More From Arcata, California
By Kevin L. Hoover

Published by
The Arcata Eye
P.O. Box 451
Arcata, California 95521-0451

news@arcataeye.com
www.arcataeye.com

Cover & chapter art by Dave Held *www.daveheld.com*

ISBN, Print ed.   0-9747662-0-8

First printing 2004

Printed in the United States of America

Library of Congress Cataloging-in-Publication Data
Hoover, Kevin L.
The Police Log : True Crime & More From Arcata, California/Kevin L. Hoover. – 1st ed.
Includes index
ISBN 0-9747662-0-8
1. Crime—Arcata (Calif.)
2. Crime—Humor.
3. Crime—Northern California.
4. Newspapers—Arcata (Calif.)
5. Newspapers—Sections, columns, etc.
6. Police—Records and correspondence.

Library of Congress Control Number: 2003099317

Table of Contents

In Memory of Larry Valadao

The Police Log
is dedicated to the
men and women of the
Arcata Police Department.

Kevin thanks Ann, Ron, Kelly, Elizabeth, Lily, Sam, Betty, Rosemary Edmiston, Terrence McNally, Cory Ratzlaff, Rebecca S. Bender, Thomas J. Doyle, Jennifer Savage, Fran Roth, Bruce Anderson, Monica Hadley, Kevin P. Klein, David Gans, all in the Well, Jim Dodge, Jon Carroll, Michelle Locke, Margie Lundstrom, Brian Sproul, Michael and Joan Brennan, Howard DeWitt, Florence Reynolds, Maggie Nystrom, Lee Wakefield, Dave Held, Seth Porges, Charmi O'Connor, the Arcata Police Department, the Arcata Volunteer Fire Department, the Arcata Historical Sites Society, Mel Brown, Floyd Stokes, Alexandra Stillman, Marcia and Simeon Tauber, Pete Villarreal, Emily Siegel, Gerry Blue, Steve Gordon, Lois and Robin Arkley, the Collenbergs, Don Kolshinski, John Antonioli, Larry Valadao, L. Scott Rebman, Pixton DuQuesne, Lenny Bruce, Frank Zappa, Mike Keneally, Ian Anderson, John Lennon and all the kindly readers who've offered encouragement along the way.

Fast Foreword

In case you happened to follow some Arcadian Rainbow to a bucket of green-gold Trainwreck nugs (a looped chorus of "Bringing in the Sheaves" providing the soundtrack) and you have only recently zombied back from the Cannabivoid, let me be the first to tell you that Kevin Hoover – publisher/editor/janitor of our excellent local weekly, the *Arcata Eye* – has attained what salivating gobs of Warholian fame-whores can only dare dream: an international cult following, many thousands strong as measured by weekly hits on the *Eye* web page, with all but two of those visiting Kevin Hoover's inspired rendering of the weekly Police Log.

The usual newspaper police report, which chronicles local law enforcement dispatches, does so in the most boring, mud-drying language imaginable, even though individual incidents are often provocative – like that mid-day scene at the notorious junction of Ninth and H, where a naked woman chased a naked man, who was riding a unicycle while waving an indigo silk scarf overhead. Such an incident deserves at least comment, and it's a mark of Kevin's particular genius that he merely does what begs doing – assuming you're willing to commit a wholesale violation of the journalistic tradition of feigning objectivity in reporting possible criminal activity.

Besides, despite occasional beacons of hope such as naked men on unicycles pursued by Beauty, the police report is dig-me-a-hole-and-roll-me-in depressing, a veritable barrage of human failings and frailties, follies and pathologies; a cavalcade of pain and sleaze and cynical hustles and soul-aching mental illness; a raw rhapsody of innocence betrayed, stolen, squandered, or otherwise lost; good will mangled and meanness magnified through hapless ignorance as well as ruthless malice. Although rage erupting from compressed desperation grabs the front page – "if it bleeds, it leads" – the police report packs its share of suffering, even if much of it results less from spectacular manifestations of evil than it does grim, constant, vacuous confusions and small collapses of morality and honor, often helpless, always petty.

If you add the police logs to national governments armed with enough nukes to totally kablooey the planet 70 times over, plus a mono-mind culture staring at screens and scarfing sugar-grease, gone way over to the grey side, a culture of blurs caught up in the Great Commodity Spectacle where it seems any minute now a siren is going to start its upward wail and never stop, life becomes grimmer. We seem to be approaching that point where going insane may be the only dignity left, but because Kevin has elevated the Police Log to an art form, he has blessedly forestalled our mental meltdown with a delightful combination of wit, imagination, and wild language, all essential components of arguably our only saving grace: laughter. Laughter, especially that directed at the self and the stars, keeps things lively, and Kevin's magical transformation of the dullest and most depressing part of a newspaper into laughter and vital understanding, replete with verbal virtuosity and inimitable style, deserves our deepest gratitude.

To say Kevin's Cop Log is entertaining is a bit like claiming Tina Turner can dance, because when he locks into his particular zone, Kevin, like Tina, can burn it down. Consider, for example, the following elevation of a routine vandalism report into a moral examination of motives, which happens to display some exquisite sonic textures and lovely prose rhythms, not to mention a biting send-up of contemporary psych-speak:

> "A squad of bike-borne vandals bashed the crap out of random objects with plastic bats as they passed through the area of Haeger Avenue and Austin Way. Perhaps, as some schools of thought hold, they were unempowered victims of a world gone mad expressing themselves as best they could in a desperate gambit to achieve personal validation and reaffirmation of selfhood. Or maybe they were just morons."

Below, in two sentences, Kevin takes a basic property damage hit-and-run, shows the personal consequences, and wraps it in a surprising mix of tech-talk and an overarching neurological metaphor:

> "One person's character deficit became another's repair bill as an unknown person of challenged driving skills interfaced with a Bayside Road fence at some

speed. The culprit's limbic system basically took over at this point, overruling the outer cortex and dictating flight from the scene."

To continue this sampling of his artistry, Kevin makes a leap of imagination into a peace-disturber's alleged thought process without even mentioning the complaint:

"This music's so righteous, everyone in the neighborhood's gonna want to hear it!"

Just for variation, another noise complaint – bongos on the Plaza – receives an overtly poetic treatment in the kick-ass anapests of the limerick, which, along with turkey vulture fledglings and octagonal lint, are among the last things one expects to find when reading a police log:

A bongo's percussory drone
Like Lucifer's own metronome
Raged on for an hour
Projecting its power
Across Patchouli Plazadome.

When Kevin first told me he was compiling a book of selections from his police logs, I admit to a doubt: I was convinced that reading pages of short takes on essentially the same subject (petty crime) could carpel-tunnel the brain and/or repetitively stress the imagination, that the individual resonance of each piece might become a drone, much like sitting down and reading an exhaustive anthology of all-star haiku, where after a few dozen you start losing the brilliance of each poem and begin hearing the homogeneity of the form, its implicit rules of attention and the required turns of mind. However, the Police Logs escape the boredom of prolonged excellence precisely because Kevin possesses the amazing ability to change the terms of engagement from item to item while turning the mind every way but loose. One way he does it – at least for me, who swoons at well-wrought neologisms – is through his inventive use of language, and especially his addition of new words. (And while I bow the deepest to Jack Spicer's assertion that the best poetry is written with an infinitely small vocabulary, neologisms at least give us more from which to choose.) I was utterly delighted when I learned that Kevin and his cohorts had decided to include a glossary to aid the reader, not only with Arcata place names and strange tribal customs, but mainly with the neologisms and slang – like nugs, plazoids and judgment-plummets, to cite three of my favorites. It seems every item carries its own small surprise – a new word, a new angle of view, a particularly felicitous phrase, an illuminating detail perfectly centered.

The *New York Press* called Kevin "a living master" of the police log form, and a recent *Editor and Publisher* (late October 2K3) deemed our own Mr. Hoover "the father" of the police log form, which is now, of course, being copied by other papers. But having read other police logs in the form Kevin opened, their inferiority is almost startling; they got the gimmick, but they woefully lack Kevin's chops. Kevin's skills and imagination impart that unmistakable print of style, that authority of voice, that is the signature of mastery. Kevin, as they say on the street, is "da kind."

Kind, however, doesn't exactly describe the moral philosophy which informs judgments often explicit in the reports, or strongly implied, as in this description: "A surfeit of multicultural diversity... blocked pedestrian passage." Or this sweet-nothing: "A... Plaza tav asked for police help in clearing up a multi-loser hairball lodged in its entrance way." "Metastasizing schlubbery..." "Festering gank pit..." You get the drift. Under the old rules of journalism, this would be considered editorializing in the news section. But Kevin ignores the rules, at least in the Police Log, although he does scrupulously adhere to a pair of operating principles: he never makes light or pokes fun at serious crime or accidents, which are covered in the news section, and he seldom uses names. If you find Kevin's moral messages a tad harsh, remember he's a newspaper editor in a small town notorious for its moral pretensions, where every day half the citizens are deriding him as a pants-wetting liberal and the other half are denouncing him as a lick-spittle running-dog of the corporate oligarchy. All this by way of issuing my own disclaimer: While I bow to Kevin's talent and admire his integrity as an editor, I don't necessarily share all his moral judgments. Many of my best friends are weirdos, whacked-outs, mouth-breathers, semi-mobile gank pits, and voidoids. So roll up some more of that 'Wreck and crush a few 40s of that hillbilly heroin and we'll ooze downtown to pus-plug the street and perhaps annoy a certain editor.

Beyond the brilliance of its individual pieces, this compilation of Kevin's best Police Logs proves greater than the sum of its parts. Taken as a whole, I was surprised to discover something I can only characterize as postmodern social realism – a radically disjointed street narrative with recurring characters (or repeat offenders) in conflict with society, each other, and themselves. And behind that story, almost overshadowed by the fun and funk, seldom mentioned, are the Arcata Police Department officers who answer every call that Kevin so artfully reports. The officers must distinguish, on the spot, benign strangeness from social danger. They break up Tavern Row fisticuffs between young men who've poured too many other intoxicants into their already plentiful supplies of testosterone. The officers hold together poor souls who are flying apart, and try to find them help. They warn, caution, counsel, and console many others, and arrest those who are a danger to us or themselves. And then fill out the paperwork. In a community where "U.S. Out of Humboldt County" is an ubiquitous bumpersticker, and one can hardly find a fan of Da Man, let's not forget that the APD behaves as peace officers should, and generally does an excellent, if thankless, job. If you still don't like them, here's what you should do: the next time you need help, dial 912. (Pardon the spontaneous degeneration into doggerel; I've been reading too many of Kevin's Police Logs lately.)

Well, speak of the dev, Kev just fired another round through the front door, demanding this Foreword I begged to write over a year ago. I should call the police, but that would be just too Arcata perfect, too full-circle juicily ironic: forced to report your own arrest. But these are strange, twisted days we live and love in, what with time folding, space warping, and winter coming on. Let me turn you over to Kevin now, confident he'll get you through.

Jim Dodge
Arcata, California
October, 2003

Jim Dodge, associate professor of English at Humboldt State University, is the author of Fup *and* Not Fade Away.

Slow Foreword

See that stuff coming out of McKinley's nose on the cover? It's cheese that really happened, and it's why I'm here in Arcata writing this.

In 1986, I had a little time off from a crummy job and wanted to get away from the San Francisco Bay Area for a few days. A friend mentioned this funky place on California's North Coast named Arcata, where his sister had attended Humboldt State University. A college town, with politics firmly rooted in the '60s, hot and cold running alternative lifestyles and lots of redwood trees, it sounded like an interesting place to spend a little time in.

Then I remembered an item I'd read about Arcata in *National Lampoon*. The humor magazine's "True Facts" column – which compiled, among other things, excerpts from small town police blotters – included this item from the *Arcata Union* newspaper:

> "Tiffany's ice cream parlor alerted police to a person defacing the statue of William McKinley on the Arcata Plaza. Police apprehended a suspect and released him with a warning not to stick cheese in McKinley's ears and nose anymore."

A town square? William McKinley with a cheese-filled nose? We headed up the coast the next morning.

Arcata, its streetside confoundments and teapot tempests, layabouts, legends, dashing politics and beautifully diverse terrain, hooked me right way. I stayed.

In 1993, I got a production job at the *Union*, started writing stuff, and was eventually asked if I wouldn't mind doing the Police Log. At that time, the "coplog" (as we called it at the paper) was a lean affair, consisting of a paltry four or five items recited almost verbatim from the Arcata Police dispatcher bulletins. I followed that form for a time, then started getting cute with it.

One day the *Union* died and not long after I started the *Arcata Eye* so I could stay here and celebrate the town's seamy underbelly and other psychic microclimes.

After getting lots of positive press for the appalling affronts to traditional journalism found in these pages, much encouragement from townsfolk, and between managing the rolling crisis of producing a weekly community newspaper, we finally got a bleedin' book together.

The basic theory of the Police Log is to tell Arcata's citizens what's going on in their town while not boring them to death. And never mind writing up every single item logged by dispatchers. The coplog is a sampling of the silliness of the streets, with context and color added to the skeletal official entries. This place being dink compared to where you live, I often know the suspects or victims in any given incident and can track them down for more groovy-grisly detail. And there's always more. Underneath the simplest two-line dispatcher summary might lurk an epic saga, possibly even cheese.

The people whose exploits populate these pages aren't all bad people who do wrong things. Most are just tempted by an opportunity to do what they gotta to grab some short-term grat. Some are just young, others may have more severe issues, and there are frequent flyers in every town. But the bulk are average folks doing things they wouldn't tell Mom about. In short, it's not who they are, but what they do that defines the true creators of these items. Just think – you too could be a sidewalk sitabout, recycling pirate or, with the right refreshments, a Fun Buncher!

A word about the Arcata Police Department: Our town is fortunate to have a PD that reflects the prevailing temperament. Cops everywhere make lightning-quick judgments with lasting consequences, routinely endure tragedy and experience stresses on a scale many of us would find very difficult to deal with. Along with this usual budget of crime, Arcata Police have to manage special situations peculiar to a fun-loving college town, from near-constant political demonstrations to locating a statue's stolen thumb. One minute they're gently coaxing an opossum out of a tree, the next they're making sure no one runs over the anti-war protesters on the Plaza – or they're reading about their difficult work in a silly limerick in the coplog.

Yes, Arcata's weird in its way, but so is everywhere else. People are people and absurdity permeates every corner of the universe. And it's all laid bare, if not barren, here in the Police Log. Mix a generous dose of goofy energy with a dash of sneaky expediency, some throbulent bongos and maybe an adult beverage or nine, and you'll soon have enough material for this, *The Police Log, True Crime & More from Arcata, California.*

Kevin L. Hoover
December, 2003

The good guys – members of the Arcata Police Department.

Photo by Terrence McNally

True Crime

• **November 13, 1995 3:15 p.m.** A 10th Street residence victimized by a recent petty theft from a porch was again depredated with the loss of a "Little Tykes" playhouse by unknown criminal masterminds.

• **May 28, 1996 10:16 p.m.** A 10th Street community recycling center reported an attempt at theft via falsification of a "buyback ticket." When recyclables are weighed out, the customer is given a ticket indicating the value of the material. The ticket is then taken over to the center's on-site second-hand store for redemption. But there's many a slip 'twixt the yard and the shop, and the sum on the ticket sometimes inflates dramatically while en route. "Periodically someone attempts to falsify the tag by adding a digit or two," explained an employee. "What usually tips us off is that they get greedy." The scam is attempted by "not just youths, but mature adults, supposedly, too," the employee explained. Center personnel now watch out for improbable sums on the tickets, and other countermeasures are in place to expose attempts at fraud.

• **December 26, 1996 2:52 p.m.** An anguished Cedar Drive woman discovered heirlooms missing from a cupboard in her home, and called police. Missing were an antique cut glass bowl, creamer and sugar bowl. "They'd been in my family for 150 years," said the woman. "You can never replace them." The victim, a senior, said she suspected a "so-called friend" of five years who had been acting as a care provider, helping her take a weekly shower. No charges have been filed, as the victim said the suspect told her she had "gotten rid" of the items. The bowl was described as half-inch thick clear cut glass eight inches across and four inches tall. The creamer and sugar bowl were each about three-by-three inches.

• **August 4, 1998 8:16 p.m.**
On Valley East, trouble arose
And evil's dark face was exposed
Unknown thieves, hearts gone hard
Entered somebody's yard
And ripped off a guy's garden hose.

• **August 6, 1998 9:40 p.m.**
An I Street market
Overheard dumpster noises
Recycling pirates!

• **September 13, 1999 8 p.m.** A Blakeslee Avenue resident's wheelchair was stolen from her front yard.

• **October 22, 1999 9:21 p.m.** If the police account is true, one gent's idea of a ripping Saturday night involves cocktail-propelled thievery at an F Street supermarket. But caught in the unforgiving glare of the store's redundant banks of fluorescent lights, he was caught and Pinked.

• **November 11, 1999 3:29 a.m.** A black-clad bungler held up a Heindon Road restaurant at knifepoint, stealing money from the reg and fleeing, but not before dropping things and leaving all kinds of fingerprints.

• **November 16, 1999 9:57 a.m.** A homebound woman gave

two blank checks to someone she knew only as "Amy." The idea was that Amy would return with food, but four days later, she hadn't been seen since.

• **January 31, 2000 10:20 a.m.** Someone grabbed a carton of cigarettes from an F Street supermarket and, burning whatever oxygen tar-encrusted lungs and nicotine-compromised hemoglobin can provide, scurried away.

• **March 13, 2000 6:44 p.m.** The hardworking crew at an I Street noodle house was deprived of their rightful tips when some cretinous parasite ripped them off.

• **May 1, 2000 11:07 p.m.** Well, *of course* her unlocked mountain bike was instantly stolen from in front of a 24-hour F Street supermarket. Goodbye, wheels; farewell, naiveté.

• **July 24, 2000 5:41 p.m.** He thought he could leave a rented rug cleaning device in the back of his pickup truck for a few minutes, and that it would be there when he got back. Now he doesn't think that.

• **August 27, 2000 6:46 a.m.** An unknown driver did a fill 'n' flee at an Alliance Road mini-mart.

• **October 11, 2000 9:06 p.m.** A bad, bad, thirsty, thirsty person ran as fast as possible away from an Alliance Road stop 'n' rob with a 12-pack under his or her arm. Shaky hands soon hoisted beer to mouth, quenching that post-heist thirst, the hastily slurped brew trickling down the thief's neck in streams which commingled with a sheen of perspiration from the running fast part.

• **October 15, 2000 8:30 a.m.** Well, they shouldn't have left that stuff in their car overnight in the 1900 block of H Street to begin with. Tough way to learn you aren't in Ohio any more.

• **October 23, 2000 3 p.m.** Though frequently anthropomorphized, an auto is merely an insensate assemblage of parts. Even the vintage red Audi into which stolen gas was pumped probably registered neither glee, guilt or thirst satisfaction as it guzzled the ill-gotten petrol while fleeing east on Giuntoli Lane.

• October 28, 2000 1:22 p.m. Did you know that there are people who cruise Arcata's streets by night, looking for easy bicycle pickings? Often fueled in their labors by nasally administered inspiration, they go for quantity. The three bikes in a garage in the 1700 block of J Street must have been quite the jackpot.

6:06 p.m. Back to the commercial district, where the male lead in our cast of *dramatis personae* next surfaced as part of an alleged fill 'n' flee at the other Valley West gas station. Thus the law – and the curtain – came down as he was citizen's-arrested on a petty theft charge, then charged with violating the terms of his own-recognizance release from imprisonment over a previous misunderstanding. Life is so complicated sometimes, though rigid Pink House routine tends to ameliorate freewill-related peril.

• October 29, 2000 3:45 p.m. Every manner of lifestyle-support gear, including backpacks, bedrolls, puppies and food boxes are commonly spotted semi-attended on the Schwazz. Randolph the traveler was surprised and disappointed to find that the total stranger he had so kindly asked to watch his shit had probably stolen same. What a stunning blow to a heart so innocent.

• November 15, 2000 3:41 p.m. She forgot, she just forgot, OK? But then she remembered, went back and paid for the gas. "My brain was going really fast," the presumed petrol purloiner, a busy graduate student and mother, later reported. "I was thinking about all kinds of things. I only went around the block and remembered."

• January 9, 2001 7:53 p.m. A bicyclist blithely left his bike unlocked on a busy street while he dashed into a video store, and the rest – including the bike – is history.

• January 27, 2001 11:59 a.m. If it isn't bolted down – with big bolts – it will be stolen. And so the picnic table outside an I Street noodle house succumbed to thieves. They'd like it back.

• March 8, 2001 11:34 a.m. By leaving his wallet in an

unlocked car on Community Park Way, a Blue Lake man donated it to a klepto artist.

• **March 11, 2001 2:47 a.m.** Two male-type persons performed a physics experiment having to do with the resistance of glass to a hurled projectile at an Alliance Road mini-mart. The punk physicists discovered that glass breaks, then ran away.

• **April 18, 2001** An innovative customer upended the traditional shopping experience at a 13th street marketplace, beginning his grocery quest by grabbing a bag and strolling down the aisles, filling it as he went. What a $50 bottle of rum couldn't accomplish, an additional $15 vessel of same surely would. And what better to guzzle one's rum with than salty snacks?

As store personnel watched the unfolding spectacle, yo-ho-ho and a bag of potato chips next went in the bag of booty, then on to the beauty department for a personal consultation. Seems the fellow's girlfriend was mad at him, or so he told the consultant. She prescribed Fairy Dirt, a fairy dust-butter admixture, two packages of which soon joined the rum 'n' chips in swelling sack. Flowers were also suggested as a relationship-healer, a concept the shopper immediately embraced. "That's #@*&! brilliant," he exclaimed, adding six irises to his loot cache.

Loaded up with life's necessities, the brazen market adventurer then sauntered to the back of the store, through an employee-only zone and onto the loading dock, where he placed the ill-gotten gains for subsequent retrieval. Swiftly, he drove up in a truck for the bag-snatch, which went awry when a store manager who'd been following the escapade finally intervened, wresting the bag from the suspect's grasp. The man then hopped in his car and raced away, only to be located a short time later in another supermarket's parking lot, where he was arrested on a charge of driving under the influence and jailed.

• **May 23, 2001 1:38 a.m.** At least a jolt won't pass through this guy from Manila's nervous system every time he sees a cop, now that the worst has already happened – he was arrested and jailed in the 1100 block of Samoa Boulevard on charges of driving with a suspended license, possession of the herb and probation violation.

• **May 31, 2001 5:27 a.m.** The always-in-Arcata traveler with the dog in a bike trailer was cited and released for camping in Larsen Park. The gentleman recently announced his opposition to vegetarianism during an impromptu oratory at a Northtown mini-mart.

9:08 a.m. Stoners chugged loco weed in the unspeakable public toilet at the Intermodal Transient Facility. When police arrived, just the sickly-sweet smell of dope smoke, commingled with urine and vandalism, remained.

• **Friday, June 1, 2001 12:59 a.m.** The folly of Plaza cig-puffing was made clear to two smokers.

12:59 a.m. Another traveler's history caught up with him at Ninth and H when police learned of the messy business down in San Ber'dino. He next spent time in Humboldt's naughty human pound.

• **June 3, 2001 8:12 a.m.** A Bayside Road resident left some stuff on her porch overnight, and of course the children's swimming vests, a Pooh Party game which was to be a gift for a 4-year-old's birthday and some other items were quickly stolen.

12:52 a.m. Some dude drained his lizard in the City's unofficial public urinal – the parking lot at Ninth and G streets.

• **June 21, 2001 2:15 p.m.** Preschoolers on a day camp outing were puzzled by a funny man who kept their teacher's frisbee after children played incorrectly and it accidentally landed in the Sacred Driveway on the south side of Stewart Park. Look, the teacher pleaded, can I just have my frisbee back? The frisbee victim exhibited rare mercy, reached into his truck and returned the straying disc. He then proceeded to aggressively photograph a helpful dad who had parked his family station wagon a foot or so inside a meaningless red zone while assisting with the children's picnic. That accomplished, the park protector retreated to his apartment to document further, similar crimes against humanity.

• **July 20, 2001 1:45–1:57 a.m.** With brain wattage likely less than that of their headlights due to inundation of the neocortex by cocktail, it may be just as well that the drivers on Samoa Boulevard and Ninth Street were hoosegowed.

• **August 12, 2001 1:45–2:16 a.m.** Stupid kidneys, don't work fast enough to make the drive home from the tavern legal.

• **August 13, 2001 4:38 a.m.** The officer and I will just stand right here while you clamber sheepishly out of the motel swimming pool.

11:04 a.m. A traveler plopped his motley baggage on the grass in front of the park bench at the Eighth and H streets Plaza corner and proceeded to make himself at home. As Monday morning traffic jostled for position at the intersection and pedestrians bustled by, the visitor to town fortified himself with swigs from a bagged bottle, hosed down the flower bed with urine and badgered passersby with unsolicited commentary.

It wasn't long before a policeman rolled up and greeted the man, who took umbrage at any suggestion that his solo encampment/ public party be curtailed. Numerous consonant-rich objections were registered as the cuffs went on, for all their vehemence barely audible above the roar of passing motorcars.

As reinforcement officers arrived, the fellow's facial hair arrangement, a heroic if somewhat undertended Van Dyke affair, bobbed in sync with an escalating chin music serenade. "Don't steal my stuff!" he commanded. "And don't plant nothin' on me! We know that's what you're all about!" Fortunately, officers disregarded his careless use of the double negative, which, if literally obeyed, might have compelled them to surreptitiously place some sort of contraband about his person.

Just before the suspect and his debonair facial hair theory disappeared into the cagelike back seat of an APD cruiser, he cobbled together a showstopper of a verbal construct which could warrant an entry in *Incarceration for Dummies*. "Satanic niggers from Hell!" he bellowed to the three non-African Americans, which caused one officer to glance at another with a, "Well, *that's* different" sort of look.

After police gathered up his scattered bags of stuff, the fellow then went to jail on public peeing and open container beefs.

The statue of William McKinley being installed on the Plaza by Byron Smith and Severn Jacobsen in 1906.

Courtesy Arcata Historical Sites Society

Big Bill as he often looks these days – gilded with politicial detritus or random objects.

Photos by Kevin L. Hoover

The Plaza

• **May 13, 1995 1 a.m.** An anonymous report came in of people climbing the heavy metal McKinley replicant on the Plaza. An officer found the President free of hangers-on.

• **May 19, 1995 9:32 p.m.** Living life to its fullest, three Friday evening revelers were smashing bottles on the Plaza, as reported by a concerned passerby. An officer contacted a group milling about in the area. Though they had no idea how the broken glass could have gotten there, the good citizens agreed to clean it up.

• **July 10, 1995 8:15 p.m.** Climbing Mt. McKinley is one thing; clambering up the massive man of metal on the Plaza is another. The presidential peak baggers were gone when officers arrived.

• November 14, 1995 5:10 p.m.
A Plaza cop took out his pen
And wrote up Food Not Bombs again
And when they saw what he had done
They spooned more soup out to someone.

• November 15, 1995 8:04 a.m. A man observed screaming at passersby near the Plaza's northeast corner told police he was venting over the loss of his wallet. It was kindly suggested that he shut up, and he did.

• November 26, 1995 7:15 p.m. A juvenile was arrested on the Plaza on suspicion of two counts of vandalism, threats to an officer, two counts of battery of a police officer and possession of tobacco, then lodged in Juvenile Hall. Next morning's sunrise found the statue of President McKinley festooned with beverage containers, old sneakers and condoms. City Parks and Recreation workers scraped it all off.

• December 11, 1995 5:38 p.m. Numerous travelers gathered at the corner of Ninth and H streets on the Plaza's northwest side, as those who wish to avoid the bustle, haste and hacky sacks sailing through clouds of cigarette smoke nearer the center of the town square often do. In this case, a corner business complained about the lingering loiterers, adding that a child among them was banging a pipe on the window. The arrival of police meant an end to the dawdlers' jollity, and they quickly dispersed. The pipe was only plastic, and had caused no harm.

• January 5, 1996 3:14 a.m.
Nighttime on the square, so enchanting
Till a man filled the air with loud ranting
Police hushed his tone
And he walked home alone
With the spirits he had been decanting.

• February 9, 1996 5:21 p.m. Out on the Plaza, dozens sat down to a hearty dinner of steaming lentil-carrot soup with chunks of potato, cucumber and sauteed onion, sopped up with baguettes. A small bongo/conga section provided the pulse as members of Food Not Bombs, homeless people and travelers, college students, children and a police officer milled about, watching each other and talking. About five gallons of soup were dispensed, consumed by scattered clutches of diners sitting about the square's flower-lined walkways.

• **April 7, 1996 1:52 a.m.** Bars closed and emptied out, filling the Plaza's northmost sidewalks with the weekend's most determined merrymakers. An officer mingled purposefully, greeting all with a nod and a smile as neon light glinted on his chestborne badge.

• **June 14, 1996 7:58 p.m.** Two men listed as travelers (but who have inhabited the Plaza and environs for as long as memory serves) were arrested for public intoxication near the site of the dead-end dust-up which had occurred moments earlier. One of the men, a self-styled peacemaker of formidable dimensions, claimed that he had inadvertently attracted police attention by involving himself in the earlier fuss. The gentle giant said that he had bear-hugged one of the scrappy fusspots to keep him from hurting himself or anyone else, and that was when police arrived.

So off to the county drunk tank it was for the admittedly tipsy man and a fellow Plazagoer, but even in the confines of his holding cell, peace proved elusive. There, he said, "One guy was sniveling pretty much" about the circumstances of his incarceration, an irritation factor exacerbated by the acoustical properties of the cell. "The echo makes it very annoying," explained the man. "If a person is loud at all, the amplification is crazy."

As the night wore on, a fresh detainee was introduced into the mix, one who listened with manifest resentment to the whiner. "I can't take all this noise," the rookie cellmate reportedly complained. "Shut up, or I'm gonna knock you out!" But the obdurate orator stayed his sniveling course, pacing the floor and acting "all aggro" about being in the lockup. At some point, the new inmate grew weary of the whimpering and finally made good on his promise of retribution. "He went over and clocked him two times in the jaw," said the witness. Correctional officers then reportedly massed outside the cell and when their number reached five, waded in to the fracas.

The two were separated, extracted and placed in isolation cells, where paradoxically, steel bars proved no barrier to a fresh spirit of fraternity. When the alleged aggressor was led away for release, the other guy reportedly called out down the hallway, "Hey brother, I'm not going to file assault charges, even though I could." Further brig bathos will go forever unrecorded, as the witness was released from custody at 2:30 a.m.

8:05 p.m. A man was spotted digging for buried treasure in the Plaza turf with the aid of a metal detector. The dirt detective said the City's Public Works department had bestowed their blessing.

• **May 28, 1997 3:08 a.m.** What Haig Patigian and George Zehndner wrought, a mere vandal managed to sully. But McKinley's bronze effigy survives, resolute and unbesmirched, standing watch over Arcata's bustle and haste.

• **October 6, 1997 5:54 p.m.** A swarm of sidewalk squatters swirled in a small eddy of hemp baubles and puppy fur in the 700 block of Ninth Street. Police cleared the clog.

• **October 8, 1997 1:40 p.m.** A nebular cluster of dogs and humans coalesced at Ninth and H streets, until a blue mass topped by a shiny star exerted a less-than-cosmic influence on the formation. It dispersed to other corners of the universe.

• **July 18, 1998 10:11 p.m.** The shot heard 'round the corner of Ninth and H streets was a bongo beat – the first of many – which compelled a nearby resident (some of the people who live on the Plaza have homes there) to the phone. An officer waded through a thigh-high thicket of plaid flannel, dog-turd dreadlocks and spacefaring bongo pilots, and the crowdlet dispersed along with any ambient percussion.

• **July 29, 1998 3:11 p.m.**
Ninth and H, "The Gauntlet"
Agglomerated humans
Moved out of the way

7:11 p.m.
Another complaint
Alleging a Gauntlet clog
Wasn't a big deal.

11:16 p.m.
This time, The Gauntlet
Lived up to its cute nickname
Twenty folks on hand.

• **August 21, 1998 2:06 a.m.** Tavern closure brings out the dark side in some Plazagoers. After allegedly kickbusting the front door of a liquor store at Ninth and H streets, police responded and found the suspect nearby enjoying a bout of fisticuffs with another fellow. The door warrior was citizen's arrested on a malicious mischief charge and was also charged with public intoxication, then taken to a place with sturdier doors.

• **September 8, 1998 10:24 a.m.**
A guy at the Ninth and G lot
Was doing what he shouldn't ought
Police were soon sent
To the Number One vent
And they cited the guy on the spot.

• **January 14, 1999 9:18 a.m.** That lame-o who visits a moral obligation on passersby to buy his stupid cigarettes for him in the name of brotherhood inspired a complaint along Tavern Row.

11:29 a.m. Shock troops of the Loser Brigade were hitting on people walking past the 800 block of Ninth Street for chump change. An octet of oblivioids scattered on cop arrival.

2:25 p.m. Over to Eighth Street, where a mob of alternative lifestylers expressed existential alienation from society by pissing all over the roadway. And away they went.

• **January 17, 1999 1:09 a.m.** A young lout bashed a window at a Plaza kitsch bar, then courageously scampered away. The bartender from the vandalized tavern chased the craven galoot and cornered him in a neighboring drinkery, but sketchy reports from the scene say capture was foiled by a large, meddlesome bystander.

· January 29, 1999 5 p.m.
Near Ninth and H, sidewalk buffoons
Were squatting and blasting loud tunes
A cop soon descended
And party time ended
For pavement patchouli poltroons.

· February 27, 1999 10:33 p.m. A philosophical divergence was expressed via fisticuffs at Ninth and H. The antagonists were jailed.

· April 23, 1999 4:59 p.m. Ninth and H'ers accumulated at Haight-Ashbury North, dismaying non-saggy portions of the populace. The millabouts meandered.

· August 7, 1999 2:02 a.m. Nimrods pounded on the outside walls of a Plaza tavern for nimrod purposes.

· August 21, 1999 9:36 p.m. A puffed-up little zero wearing medium-size headphones and a full-size speech impediment kept charging into Plaza bars and acting not unlike a butthead. After a we-mean-business sidewalk takedown and an ill-received warning, police were notified, but the nuisance had by then abated.

· September 8, 1999 7:32 p.m. Dried animal skin pulled taut over a tapered cylinder. This implement, coupled with rhythmic hand impacts, forms the basis of one person's mellow trance and another's merciless torture. Especially on the Schwazz.

· September 27, 1999 8:18 p.m. A taxidermy-oriented Plaza tav asked for police help in clearing up a multi-loser hairball lodged in its entrance area.

· October 1, 1999 1:47 a.m. Guests at a Plaza hotel apparently had a low threshold for seething masses of gibbering cocktail enthusiasts outside their windows as the bars flushed out. A kindly lieutenant won the crowd over with his smile, and soon all was down to a dull roar.

• **October 2, 1999 1:23 a.m.** A guy whizzed in the alley behind Tavern Row, under which a block-long urine plume must be expanding into the water table.

• **October 22, 1999 5:47 p.m.** Imperious importuners were asked not to berate passersby for pocket change on the Plaza.

• **October 27, 1999 12:31 p.m.** Someone thought they saw a weirdo on the Plaza, but this couldn't be verified.

• **October 28, 1999 2:54 a.m.** Two men playing in the vomit/urine-redolent alley behind the 800 block of Ninth Street were asked to clean up the mess and "cease their activities until daytime."

• **November 1, 1999 1:51 a.m.** A Westhaven man was arrested in the 800 block of Ninth Street for allegedly flashing what turned out to be a fake gun. He was taken to a real jail.

• **New Year's Day 2000 12:20 a.m.** A woman plummeted to earth from atop a Plaza statue, but was unharmed, or at least feeling no pain.

• **January 21, 2000 8:14 p.m.** A clutch of indolents wallowing in the spittle and cigarette butt encrusted sidewalk in front of Tavern Row skedaddled at the sight of a crisply attired APD emissary.

• **January 23, 2000 9:31 p.m.** A Plaza tavern distinguished by numerous glass-eyed exhibits of the taxidermist's art suffered a multi-hairball pile-up at its entrance. A quick call to gendarmes and the congestion vanished.

• **January 27, 2000 1:20 a.m.** It's not as though the standards for late-night comportment at a Plaza sports bar are all that complicated or stringent, and yet, one local fellow just didn't make the grade. He won't be back.

• **February 13, 2000 8:27 p.m.** After allegedly accusing a kindly Plaza shop employee of poisoning his food, a man was said to have lingered in the business, ostentatiously placing his hand inside his shirt and staring at another employee, as if fondling a weapon of some kind. The incident was documented.

• **February 16, 2000 2:31 p.m.** Numerous folks frolicked morosely at Ninth and H, annoying passersby with the "Spare change to feed my puppy?" gambit. They dispersed on an officer's arrival.

• **April 13, 2000 9:08 p.m.** A person deemed unfit to inhabit a near-Plaza tavern retaliated by slamming his transportation – a curved, tapered board with wheels – against the business' outside wall. Then, having taught the inert edifice a lesson, he rolled away.

• **April 19, 2000 8 - 8:28 p.m.** Intake/excrete problems infested the sidewalk along Tavern Row. First, a traveler was busted on a public intox/public urination charge, then a while later, another travelin' man was arrested on a public intox/open container charge. Perhaps they compared notes on their respective fluid transfer specialties and the injustice of it all in the Pink House, where both were booked and lodged.

• **May 23, 2000 4:53 p.m.** Ninth and H'ers took semi-furtive puffs off a reefer at Ninth and H. When police arrived, only technically dopeless squinters were on hand.

• **May 24, 2000 8:33 a.m.** Ninth and H: This one dude was all, like, let's fight, and this other dude, he was all, y'know, like, *no way*.
So the first dude goes aggro and starts wailin' on the other dude and then the pigs came and he was like, *so* outta there... allegedly.

• **June 2, 2000 1:22 p.m.** A traveler tried to make a little money selling grungy hemp and bead doodads on the Plaza, but that old business license thing came up again.

• **June 13, 2000 11:09 a.m.** The joy of self-administered lung cancer-inducing treatments was tempered somewhat for a Plazagoer, who was warned by an officer.

• **June 15, 2000 11:26 p.m.** Some guy's writhing face-hole erupted with halitosis-borne verbiage that made up in volume for what it lacked in decency at Ninth and H streets. A brush with adult beverages preceded the event.

• **June 28, 2000 7:26 p.m.** A brassy climber mounted McKinley.

• **July 11, 2000 1:58 a.m.** A Kneeland man didn't cope too well with the tragedy of closing time at a near-Plaza tavern. Vandalism and public intox were the charges; the tav and a nearby business were the victims; the Pink House was his destination.

• **July 18, 2000 11:43 p.m.** His goal was simple: obtaining the pocket contents of passerby. The method was ineffectual: asking. The man was encouraged to leave the entrance to a Plaza hotel.

• **July 24, 2000 7:21 p.m.**
Jeremiah, a traveling bloke
Sat right down and fired up a smoke
His Plaza location
Soon brought him frustration
Curtailing his nicotine tokes.

• **August 2, 2000 3:05 p.m.** A parcel of scrounge lizards encumbered egress at a Plaza chiropractic center.

11:15 p.m. Planet wanderers clashed over nothingness along Tavern Row. Two disputatious chappies were deemed too pickled for public perambulation, and were promptly plopped in Pink.

• **August 20, 2000 5:05 p.m.** A Plaza seller of little twisty hemp doohickeys and glass pipes for ingestion of herbal blends was warned about business license requirements.

• **August 22, 2000 5:29 p.m.** Another small business owner on the Plaza works under a constant siege of scroungeloids milling about in the doorway of his shop. He called police, but the cloud of saggy-clad slumpers had schlepped away by then.

9:15 p.m.
A copper thought something amiss
Observing a lass take a piss
On view, indiscreet
At Ninth and H street
A ticket impinged bladder bliss.

• **September 7, 2000 11:34 a.m.** Arthur the traveler enjoyed an adult beverage along Tavern Row. Maybe the Temperance League's water fountain was full of vomit again, leaving him no choice.

• **September 16, 2000 9:46 p.m.** Were you to compile imagery and lore of Earth for broadcast to distant civilizations elsewhere in the cosmos, it is doubtful your data stream would include the inconclusive slapfest among travelers along Tavern Row.

• **September 18, 2000 5:06 p.m.** Vestigial brainstem impulses barely managed to motate several sitabouts from the doorway of a near-Plaza business.

• **September 22, 2000 5:36 p.m.** "Hey, want a handmade hemp necklace? Need any nugs?" asked the casually dressed gent at Ninth and H. Appearance of a cop car ended sales for the day.

• **October 6, 2000 7:44 p.m.** A little herd of scrounge lizards near the Plaza did not realize they were milling about in the middle of a walkway used by people who have somewhere to go in life. Requests that they move out of the way only overwhelmed their THC-clotted reasoning processes with a data glut of abstract concepts. What they did understand was a scary blue uniform and shiny badge, and soon the sidewalk was clear.

- **October 8, 2000 3:45 p.m.** Some 25 to 30 idlers exchanged hugs, nugs, folklore and casual infections at the desolate Ninth and H corner. Police forged an agreement that the sidewalk should at least be kept clear for the passing parade.

- **October 10, 2000 4:10 p.m.** A Plaza merchant forwarded numerous customer reports of metastasizing schlubbery on both sides of Ninth and H streets. An officer cruised the festering gank pit and found nothing awry.

- **October 11, 2000 8:51 p.m.** Had the small group who clogged a taxidermy-intensive social establishment been model railroading aficionados, their relocation would have required much painstaking disassembly of intricately joined track, tiny trestles, Lilliputian landscape ornaments and other scale miniatures like bonzai'd ornaments on a dry-wobble landscape. As it happened, though, the doorway blockers' chosen avocation was standing around and smoking, so the move was relatively rapid and painless.

- **October 16, 2000 12:28 p.m.** A parcel of scroungeloids befestered Ninth and H. An officer parked his car nearby, prompting what was probably the most purposeful activity on the part of those in the area the whole day – a brisk walk elsewhere.

- **October 17, 2000 4:49 p.m.** Scroungeloid spacefarers descended to Earth slightly east of their usual Ninth and H streets-area base of operations. An officer acting as a representative of terrestrial civilization made contact and the crew set a course westward ho to the mother ship across the Plaza.

- **October 29, 2000 12:56 a.m.** Just think, you too could have been part of the impromptu gathering of acquaintances in the alley behind Tavern Row. Membership in the tight-knit circle was exclusive to anyone who happened to show up and who knew how to do that brotherhood-verifying, three-part righteous power handshake. The cop cruiser wasn't entirely unexpected, and the alley cats knew the Pink House avoidance drill: smile and disperse amenably.

• **November 6, 2000 12:03 a.m.** The distinction between sidewalk and street blurred, along with every other aspect of consciousness, for they who populate Ninth and H streets day and night. A concerned motorist reported her progress through the intersection hampered, and an officer acted as human Drano on the hirsute habitues, removing the collective clog.

• **November 10, 2000 11:38 a.m.** In what might be viewed as a macro-scale implementation of Brownian Motion, scroungelings milled pointlessly at Ninth and H. A blue man greeted them, bringing purpose, albeit temporary, to their young lives.

5:51 p.m. Impedimentarians did what they do best, and you know where.

6:54 p.m. A drunk with little grasp of either subtlety or discretion, not to mention common decency, took a whiz right on the wall a few feet from the entrance to a Plaza tavern. An off-duty firefighter more experienced both with nozzle control and propriety happened to be passing by with his wife en route to a nearby restaurant, and notified police. The amateur hydrologist was found in a local tavern and left with friends. "We rarely frequent the Plaza, just because of that kind of thing," the witness said.

• **November 14, 2000 5:52 p.m.** They weren't the first tents on the Plaza, but these shelters were to keep the rain off cameras, not hobos.

• **November 16, 2000 11:52 a.m.** A traveler who never goes anywhere but here got into an argument with whoever was passing by at Sixth and H, a major south-of-Plaza weirdo throughput vector.

• **November 25, 2000 2:45 p.m.** Sidewalk socialites at Ninth and H exchanged witty banter, which in their case involved monosyllabic grunts and demonstrative gestures. Police helped reduce the denizens' density.

• **November 26, 2000 7:26 p.m.** Ninth and H quasi-residents used a traffic cone to block the street so as to importune passing motorists for their spare change. An officer restored normalcy, after a fashion.

• **November 28, 2000 1:58 a.m.** Unspecified creatures ignited firecrackers and bonked bongos on the Plaza, which conflicted with the interests of hotel lodgers. The forces of annoyance were skulking when officers arrived.

• **December 4, 2000 12:56 p.m.** Anti-Christmas forces grinched holiday decorations on the Plaza.

• **December 9, 2000 7:12 a.m.** A reported weirdo on the Plaza couldn't be found, or at least singled out.

• **December 16, 2000 1:49 a.m.** Combatants became fistical at Ninth and H, but found common ground in their decision to flee at the sight of a cop car. One slow-to-motate chap lingered, and, in classic devil-take-the-hindmost fashion, was arrested on a public drunkenness charge and jailed.

• **January 9, 2001 9:55 p.m.** A guy was so looped outside a Plaza refreshment dispensary that the complexities of staving off Earth's gravitational pull eluded him. A vestigial and underutilized upper extremity – his head – was the loser in a close encounter with the pavement, and he was ambulanced to the hospital.

• **January 12, 2001 1:41 p.m.** Skaters got in some grind 'n' go on the Plaza flower beds.

• **January 20, 2001 1:25 a.m.** Back-alley hangabouts behind Tavern Row exchanged differing opinions by the fistful. But overriding their mutual anathema was the loathing of all things cop, as embodied in the blue and white that hove to. The combatants scampered.

• **January 22, 2001 6:51 p.m.** Ninth and H'ers exercised their constitutional right to play drums and threaten people who erroneously thought they had the right to walk by without being called names.

- **February 12, 2001 1:12 p.m.** A young mumbler who is forfeiting his mandate to become a loyal plastic robot for a world that doesn't care instead hangs around near metal and plastic robot cash-dispensing machines, sullenly importuning users from beneath a pulled-down wool cap. He slumped away to another ATM.

- **February 17, 2001 12:27 a.m.** A Eureka man was arrested at Ninth and H on charges of public drunkenness and probation violation, while an Arcata 18-to-21'er was arrested on charges of lying to police about who he was and having totally bogus I.D. The tippler went to Big Pink; the identity crisis went home to mommy.

10:20 a.m. A Hayforker became swept up in the excitement of big city life and had words with someone in front of a Plaza night club.

- **February 25, 2000 6:29 p.m.** A Plaza no-no sign – the one at Ninth and H – was uprooted, wrapped in an abandoned garment and tossed on the grass. After a photographer took a picture, a nearby sitabout expressed disgust with the vandalism, saying, "It makes us all look bad," and replaced it. The loosely anchored sign was again tossed aside the next morning, photographed, replaced and so on.

- **March 1, 2001 12:40 a.m.** A putative party boy made a big splash on the nightclub scene with his allegedly drunken brain, pocketful of no-no's and the big drama production in the entranceway. He was soon the life of the Pink House.

- **March 6, 2001 7:21 p.m.** Lingerers with chemical bravado bothered passersby at Ninth and H, then scuttled.

- **March 13, 2001 11:12 a.m.** The Ninth and H streets sidewalk was overcapacity with folks using it to go absolutely nowhere. Fuzz warned fuzzies.

• **March 18 7:14 p.m.** Downtown ATMs are becoming places where needy strangers introduce themselves.

10:52 p.m. A short-lived but attention-getting interpersonal upheaval at Ninth and H streets brought official attention.

• **March 19, 2001 2:36 p.m.** Ninth and H'ers did what they do best – loitered, building memories, but only for the near-future, due to short-term memory loss.

6:20 p.m. A traveler's idea of a good time may differ from yours, and certainly varies from community standards – he got an early start on his party weekend by, police say, driving drunk, driving with an open container, possession of marijuana while motoring and driving on a suspended license. Next, an express flight from Dirt Merchant Central to the Pink House, courtesy APD Airlines.

• **March 29, 2001 1:24 a.m.** A party animal allegedly behaving beastly in front of a Plaza night club was asked to go away.

2:23 a.m. But did he listen? No. Party Beast was at it again at the club, and was arrested, charged with being a boy in a man's world and jailed.

• **March 30, 2001 Late report** A traveler's Bic-flickin', cig-suckin' nic-fit on the Plaza ended with a cop-greetin', code-quotin' cite-signin', butt-grindin' denouement.

• **April 14, 2001 2:31 a.m.** Things got ugly in front of a downtown doughnut shop. A youth was arrested on a charge of fighting and released to mommy, an adult was Pinked on a charge of public sloshage.

• **June 14, 2001 11:34 a.m.** A traveler was observed placing posters described as offensive on a statue of a president on the Plaza. She agreed to take them down.

• **July 16, 2001 1:37 a.m.** Future historians may plumb the ontogeny of the shouty man-spat on the Plaza, but probably they won't, because it was just really, really stupid.

2:43 p.m. In the movies, combatants are choreographed to climactic triumph or humiliation. At Ninth and H, drunkenly programmed knuckle bouquets generally travel on misguided trajectories, merely grazing a targeted jaw and ineffectually impacting the grimy chainlink at the site, and so on until one of the gladiators has the presence of mind to vomit on his adversary, leaving him vanquished by volcanic viscera.

• **July 19, 2001 2:24 a.m.** Trouble in donutville, but ejection of a problematic pastry aficionado restored morale.

9:14 p.m. Pilferage takes a toll on any retail establishment's bottom line and ability to offer quality, affordable services to its neighborhood.

3:56 p.m. Arcata, the land of public therapy, where an outgoing chappie tripped the dark fantastic at Ninth & H to little apparent avail.

8:32 p.m. Ninth and H, more ventertainment.

• **July 21, 2001 6:08 p.m.** If you knew just *how darn mad* this guy gets at the world, you might better understand why he had no choice but to circle the Plaza in his car, yelling at folks to discharge his pent-up frustrations. This is why the Lord invented decoupage, model railroading and game shows.

• **August 13, 2001 4:21 p.m.**
O Ninth and H, where is thy soul?
Your spawn rock on beyond control
They sprawl and skate and cadge and creep
The mall with the asbestos heap.
Looped on the Kind they stand abuzz
Till tiffy townies phone the Fuzz
Who co-star with the dazed/confused
In one more scene from *Ninth Street Blues.*

Mindbenders

- **April 28, 1994 7:57 p.m.** An I Street business reported a group of intoxicated persons playing basketball in their parking lot. Police contacted three allegedly drunken dunkers, finding them sober sportsmen and not the bibulous dribblers they were reported to be. Case closed.

- **December 1, 1994 6:45 p.m.** An employee of a G Street market reported a man having left a shopping bag containing marijuana inside the business. While an officer was en route, the careless contraband carrier came back, went behind the counter, nabbed the bag and left. The officer caught up with him on the nearby pedestrian overpass, and cited him for a drug violation.

- **February 19, 1995 10:50 p.m.** Activated alarms brought police to a Sunny Brae dental office. Unknown suspects had attempted to force a door to a room where nitrous oxide is stored.

- **March 7, 1995 4:34 p.m.** A Redwood Hall resident reported a man approaching her on the Quad and asking if she wanted a "contract to smoke marijuana in the residence halls." The cannabis contractor couldn't be located.

• **September 22, 1995 6:51 p.m.** A Redwood manor resident reported a man with bushy hair and a beard asking him if he "ate mushrooms." Police couldn't find the curious subject.

• **November 3, 1995 5:33 p.m.** A helium tank used to fill balloons in a Valley West variety store proved an irresistible lure to area children, who, to the dismay of an employee, could not be dissuaded from coming in and taking hits off the thing. The gas-gorged youths were gone when police arrived.

• **November 10, 1995 2:15 a.m.**
An earwitness described a loud clank
From a car on Alliance Road's bank
It had crashed and then coasted
Participants, toasted
Found repose in the county drunk tank.

• **November 18, 1995 12:01 a.m.** An impending disturbance brewing in a large crowd waiting for the midnight movies drew police to a G Street theater. Youth instigators in a large crowd waiting to see cult comedy classic *Up In Smoke*, which depicts the tiresome misadventures of two wacky, substance-dependent buffoons, were pointed out to police.

• **January 22, 1996 3:55 p.m.** An H Street resident looked out his window, noticing two men lurking nearby. One of the men, who the resident said was carrying a lunch bag and acting "sneaky," reportedly said, "Do you know anybody that might want to buy some?" The other man's reply was unintelligible, but he then reportedly looked in Mr. Sneaky's bag and exclaimed, "Mushrooms!" With that, the resident called police, reasoning that "People don't get that excited about shiitakes." An officer arrived shortly, but the furtive fungus fanciers had fled. "I don't like drugs going on around my home," said the resident.

• **January 26, 1996 8:32 p.m.** A knock on the door of a

Westwood Court apartment interrupted the "corny" movie a resident and her friend were watching. Answering the door, the resident was confronted by a woman who had once panhandled a relative outside the building with a "sob story." The woman, who did not appear threatening, announced, "I'm an idiot. Do you have a quarter?"

Though compelling, the appeal failed to sway the resident to cut loose with any funds. "I said 'no' and shut the door," she reported.

She said she then watched out the window as the woman proceeded to a home across the street, where she apparently succeeded in obtaining a handout. Next stop was an adjacent mini-mart, from which the purposeful panhandler soon emerged carrying a paper bag. Curious, the resident went over and quizzed a store employee as to the nature of the woman's purchase. It was beer, she was told.

• **January 30, 1996 8:22 a.m.** A purse left in the recreation hall at a G Street apartment complex was opened by the manager, who was looking for identification. Inside was regular purse stuff and a "small decorative jelly jar" full of marijuana. The herb-laden handbag was turned in to police. Meanwhile, the owner returned to the apartment building's office, asking for the purse, and was told it was in the hands of the law. "She turned and walked out very unhappily" at the news, said the apartment manager. The purse was later returned to the woman, sans grass, and police action will swiftly ensue. "I'd like for people to know that we don't tolerate that," the manager said.

• **February 3, 1996 9:12 p.m.** An anonymous complaint of beer cans hurtling into the street from a South G Street residence drew officers, who found a birthday celebration in progress. The hostess, who had just turned 24, denied culpability for the high-octane canisters strewn about. "It was King Cobra, for crying out loud," she protested. "I wouldn't drink that if you paid me!" The woman and her public-spirited guests volunteered to clean up the cans between quaffs of Guinness. "I've had a lot of negative contact with law enforcement officials," said the woman, a veteran of various high-profile countercultural events in town. "I was surprised at how nice they [Arcata Police] were."

10:33 p.m. When robust noise levels at the party annoyed a neighbor a few houses down, another kindly policeman came and peeled off a warning notice.

• **April 23, 1996 12:16 a.m.** If there's pot possibly in your pocket and booze believed to be in your bloodstream, make sure your stereo blasts the neighbors out of their beds in the midnight hour. That way, policemen will come around and check you out. This sure-fire prescription for jail time was pioneered by a Union Street apartment dweller.

Actual high-tech Arcata pot.

Photo by Kevin L. Hoover

· June 20, 1998 8:15 p.m.
As Crabs beat upon Meadowlarks
Drunko dopes shouted purple remarks
Cops talked with the fans
Of profanity bans
And the beer-glutted goons left the park.

· July 10, 1998 6:31 p.m.
The HSU walkway drew Fuzz
To pick up a traveler because
They say he was smashed
With a cannabis stash
In jail he sat out his buzz.

· July 23, 1998 9:15 p.m.
Psst, buddy – yes, *you* – over here
Would you come in and buy us some beer?
The traveler agreed
Met the juveniles' need
And off they drove with bubbly cheer.

· July 25, 1998 1:04 a.m. A liquorish visitor from Santa
Barbara found swerving around at Giuntoli Lane and Valley West
Boulevard was treated to a free stay in Big Pink.

· October 7, 1998 3:28 p.m. Afternoon cocktails disrupted the
stride of a man at Eighth and H streets, alarming a passerby.

· November 18, 1998 1:56 - 3:07 a.m.
Downtown, police hauled
Cocktail enthusiasts
Off to the Pink House.

· December 23, 1998 4:19 p.m.
Hey, here's some money
Could you buy us some brewskis?
Move along now, kids.

• **February 9, 1999 11:20 a.m.**
A Ninth and H guy, rather silly
Put bottle to lips, took a swilly
In cuffs he soon left
Deemed 647(f)
The stewed dude was stinko-Pinked, schwilly.

• **March 11, 1999 2:50 a.m.**
Encumbered by cocktail funk
A guy at the Marsh passed out drunk
Though outside the rule
A cop who was cool
Let slumber the liquor-logged lunk.

• **March 17, 1999 6:27 p.m.** *"Omigod, I'm so stoned,"* the young woman confessed to a store clerk and random customers at a Samoa Boulevard market. "I've never smoked anything like that – I have to remind myself every two seconds to stay awake. Can I use your phone?" Out in the parking lot, a man appeared to be waiting for her to come out of the store, and was relating the totality of the young woman's intoxication to amuse passersby. A concerned cat food purchaser notified police, and they paid a call. By then, the girl's mom was there to save and scold her young libertine.

• **April 30, 1999 11:50 p.m.**
Alone a man sat
At Fifth and F streets
After a booze interlude.
Holding his head in his hands
Assistance declined.

• **July 4, 1999 3:51 p.m.** A card-carrying medical marijuana patient was smoking a fatty at the 4th of July Jubilee on the Plaza, and, he says, passed the psychoactive stogie to anther patient without looking, but the next toke was taken by a non-certified cannabis fancier instead. The cardless cannabis consumer was cited for possession, and the medical user was cited for providing marijuana – "Southern Light" and "Train Wreck" varieties, to be specific – to another.

• **August 14, 1999 1:43 a.m.** A chap in Room 111 put something illegal in his mouth and swallowed it, thinking perhaps that it might make him very, very happy. Or profound. Or cosmic. Instead, he became just another bummed-out howling raver scraped from a value-priced motel room and delivered into the Inhospitable Arms – the county slammer.

• **August 22, 1999 1:58 a.m.** Two men, no strangers to refreshing adult beverages, went to a friend's apartment in the 1100 block of G Street. He wasn't there, so, utilizing cocktail logic, they decided to break in. Someone noticed this and told police, who in turn advised the duo to wait patiently on the porch for their friend to arrive home.

• **September 10, 1999 1:37 p.m.** A special person guzzled a large brew by the Post Office, shrewdly calculating that by concealing the beer bottle in a paper bag and drinking from it, authorities would be baffled. They weren't. An officer asked if it was beer, and took the bag/bottle for a verifying sniff. Thirsty boy then demonstrated true genius by trying to grab back the open container from the officer whilst serenading him with the more guttural portions of his three-figure vocabulary. Numerous officers subdued the determined drinker, who was taken to the Pink House on charges of having an open container, resisting arrest and being a belligerent jackass.

• **September 30, 1999 9:07 a.m.** Adult male leisure experts chugged breakfast joints outside the entrance to the ball park.

• **October 1, 1999 2:47 a.m.** Semi-feral goodtimers in the night exchanged primitive, alcohol-blurred hoots and grunts down at the Marsh, where they shouldn'ta been anyway.

8:23 a.m. Several hooch-addled humans were discovered sprawled along the Marsh trail from South H Street, with wheelchairs parked nearby. An officer warned them about littering. He also warned an addressless person and someone from Kneeland about camping.

• **October 14, 1999 3:40 a.m.** Make friends with Mr. Cocktail and you might find yourself trying to open your neighbor's front door instead of your own. A policeman helped navigate the wayward beverage hobbyist home.

• **November 4, 1999 8:20 a.m.** Some big bags of shake – marijuana trimmings too THC-deprived to bother with – were found in the 600 block of 10th Street. An officer snatched them up.

• **January 17, 2000 5:15 p.m.** Lawn decor in the 500 block of H Street included an alcohol-defuncted Eureka man. Awakened, he offered a wordy but largely incomprehensible explanation for the events leading up to his shrubbery siesta, then he wandered away.

• **January 20, 2000 2:02 a.m.** Beer 'n' pot, or so the cops say. The guy went to Big Pink.

• **February 24, 2000 2:34 p.m.** A man was arrested at Ninth and I streets and jailed on charges of "selling bunk in lieu/controlled substance" and probation violation. The pseudope – "coke," he reportedly said it was – had been offered to someone who chose not to put chemicals proffered by a stranger on a streetcorner into his body and experience the resultant benefits to his health and well being. The sales-resistant customer called police on his cell phone and kept the alleged amateur pharmacist in sight until officers arrived. The suspect was found with four bagged samples of white powder, which he told police was a mixture of baking soda and salt; enough to make one's nostrils cringe just thinking about it. Turns out selling fake illegal drugs is a felony, just like the real thing.

• **March 27, 2000 8:24 a.m.** A Fieldbrook man allegedly equipped for a wake 'n' bake was cited for marijuana possession in Stewart Park.

• **April 16, 2000 1:54 a.m.** Alleged driving while stinko, driving with a suspended license-o, probation vio and no proof of insuro led to an evening in Pinko for a man of unknown address at Sixth and H.

• **April 20, 2000 6:30 p.m.** One of many travelers was cited and released for peeing in Redwood Park. Rejecting traditional hierarchical values and fascistic hygiene standards, the annual impromptu 420 wingding was not organized by any one person or organization. Thus, no permit was obtained nor porta-potties deployed, leaving 800 people with just two massively overtaxed and skanky restrooms, plus the woods in which to whiz.

• **April 24, 2000 1:07 p.m.** Wait – isn't marijuana supposed to make you mellow and disinterested in conflict? To the Pink House with you, o tempestuous toker!

• **May 12, 2000 8:42 a.m.** Now that the pernicious influence of marijuana has been removed from his lifestyle, perhaps the traveler found at the Intermodal Transient Facility can reassemble his weed-shattered existence.

• **July 25, 2000 12:35 a.m.** Morons bellowed guttural grunts – and, no doubt, waved their arms around a lot – by way of a primitive, ineffectual attempt at mammal-to-mammal communication at Sixth and H. Miraculously, the gibbering stumblebums managed to wander from the scene without mortal injury to themselves before police arrived.

• **August 8, 2000 7:19 p.m.** Another bag changed hands at Ninth and H streets, right in front of God, a passing police log writer and everybody.

• **August 17, 2000 11:37 p.m.** A man took to screaming in an F Street alley. He was arrested on a charge of severe cocktail engorgement and taken to the Pink House.

• **August 19, 2000 2:53 a.m.** Police say the 10th and J street drunk driver lacked sufficient cognitive assets to pilot a ton-and-a half-of metal, plastic and flammable liquid around town. Off to the Pink House drunk tank.

3:57 a.m. This other dude's brainstem was chemically retarded by grown-up beverages and an unspecified controlled substance, police say. He went from Giuntoli Lane at Valley West Boulevard to Big Pink.

• **August 31, 2000 1:15 a.m.** A guy at a bar bothered some people, then wandered away to further insignificant endeavors. Call it a lifestyle choice.

• **September 7, 2000 12:13 a.m.** This guy had a few more solar orbits to go before his blood alcohol could be at this particular level, especially while driving. Another funster pickled in Pink.

• **September 10, 2000 2:42 a.m.** The products of the brewer's art precipitated a judgment plummet for an alleged driver at 11th and K streets. After police hacked through the fog of alcohol funk issuing from a glistening horizontal fissure on the lower front portion of his face (which also made ineffectual exculpatory noises), they discovered his other "motorist's helper" – a special smoking blend.

3:59 p.m. Paul and Amanda's planetary wanderings brought them to the maze-like aisles of a 13th Street marketplace, where employees were impressed by the couple's spirited demeanor, if little else.

• **September 16, 2000 8:48 a.m.** A man enjoying an adult breakfast at Ninth and H streets was cited for having an open container.

• **September 29, 2000 1:58 - 2:50 p.m.** Stoners too dopey to see the cop coming were cited and released for pot possession in Redwood Park.

• **October 7, 2000 8:46 p.m.** A bibulator with a flask voluntarily lined the gutter with its prized contents.

• **October 8, 2000 2:01 a.m.** A traveler reprised the role of Jack Lemmon in the 1962 cinema classic *The Days of Wine and Roses*; specifically the scene where desperate alcoholic Joe Clay pounded futilely on the door of the closed liquor store. Though the full bottles of sweet, sweet liquor cruelly mocked him from the other side of the glass, his need was not to be fulfilled and he wandered away.

• **October 13, 2000 12:57 a.m.** Some under-21ers' recombinant alcohol/automotive research yielded easily reproducible results for young field experimenters on L.K. Wood Boulevard at the Sunset Avenue overhead.

• **October 16, 2000 5:40 p.m.** A graduate of Cocktail College found at Ninth and H pursued postgraduate studies at the Pink House.

6:41 p.m. A Laurel Drive resident paid inadvertent homage to Frank Zappa when an anonymous caller invoked his coinage and described a cocktail-modified neighbor as "freaking out." The beverage victim was able to care for herself, and agreed to be quiet. She's really very groovy, but forgive her 'cause she's stoned.

• **October 18, 2000 10:24 p.m.** Another cocktail hobbyist was transplanted from Ninth and H to a Pink House cell, which seemed to spin like a not-so-merry-go-'round.

• **October 22, 2000 12:42 - 1:40 a.m.** Tangy grownup-style beverages triggered a cause-and-effect chain of events culminating in several souls awakening spinning in a Pink House remove with bunkmates of fresh and short-lived acquaintance.

• **October 28, 2000 8:31 a.m.** Two chaps cloistered in the entrance alcove of a Plaza shop enjoyed each others' company whilst familiarizing themselves with containers of hops-based liquid breakfast. Fortified for the day, they tottered off.

• **November 2, 2000 1:16 a.m.** A Eureka man was arrested on a felony warrant, and also charged with parole violation possession of the ingredients of a happy, healthful, fulfilling life – a controlled substance and the hypodermic needle with which to jab it in.

• **November 8, 2000 10:43 a.m.** A nug vendor offered cannabinoid-laden marijuana buds, or possibly just to take his money and disappear under the guise of same, to a disinterested person at Ninth and H streets.

5:24 p.m. Career indolents milled at Ninth and H streets, their ranks surging as they met to negotiate nug exchanges, then ebbing as the furtive transactions took place in alleys and elderly autos parked nearby. If you don't know what a nug is, well, you just aren't smoking enough dope.

• **November 9, 2000 12:39 p.m.** A fuzzy proffered nuggets to the wrong person at Eighth and H, and police were called. The budding salesman was gone, way.

• **November 28, 2000 5:25 p.m.** Needy, weedy scruffmuffins offered unforgiving appraisals of a passerby's character when he declined their requests for money at Ninth and H. That doesn't seem very fair.

• **December 4, 2000 8:01 a.m.** Young pink lungs withered and turned brown under the onslaught of cigarette smoke. An officer forestalled the gaseous corruption by relieving the kids of their smokes.

• **December 9, 2000 3:04 p.m.** Cocktails fueled the rhetorical passions of an adult beverage enthusiast at Ninth and H streets, and the ingestion of same led to various high-vol utterances which made up in decibels what they lacked in coherence.

• **December 18, 2000 4:55 p.m.** A possibly intoxigoofied person was reported marooned in the bus station bathroom. A friend was called to come and pick him up.

• **December 28, 2000 6:17 p.m.** During a lull between customers, a Plaza liquor store clerk glanced over by the newspaper rack and noticed a large white plastic bag. A peek inside revealed the kind of groundscore many fine citizens can only dream of, and surely do – three to four pounds of smiling marijuana. Police were summoned, and no less than four cruisers responded. The big bonus bag o' shake was seized for destruction. Impish officers reportedly took the bag across the street and showed it to the crowd at Ninth and H, asking "Did anyone lose this?" But there were no takers, likely because the sight of the mega-stash temporarily disabled their speech mechanisms. As to the mystery of the bonus bag's appearance, the store employee speculated that its former owner may have had other things on – or in – his mind. "I think he was so wiped he just forgot it," the clerk-criminalist surmised.

• **January 6, 2001 4:57 p.m.** Today's astute stoner should probably not pack more than an ounce of wacky terbacky, then try and tell a clear-eyed policeman he's someone other than who he really is. The remainder of mystery man's enfeebled buzz was completely expunged by the clanging doors and harsh fluorescent lighting of the Pink House.

• **January 12, 2001 6:47 p.m.** Adult potions, laced with THC and stirred with jail bars, comprised an evening's heady entertainment fare for one traveler near Ninth and H.

• **January 15, 2001 12:22 a.m.** Possession of marijuana, possession of alcohol, possession of a driving-impairing liquor buzz. These are the things that make Arcata Police officers grow a big ol' frown. Being from Visalia is somewhat excusable.

• **January 17, 2001 1:36 p.m.** A sidewalk socialite ingested THC outside the hardware store.

• **January 19, 2001 8:08 p.m.** Whatever happened to putting a frog in someone's pocket, taping a sign to their back, or putting gum on a seat? These kids were arrested on charges of public intoxication, marijuana possession and resisting arrest at 10th and J streets. Which is worse – Juvenile Hall or Dad and Mom?

• **February 9, 2001 7:23 p.m.** The power of the cocktail was harnessed to propel a man from the 1500 block of G Street to the Pink House.

• **March 19, 2001 2:36 p.m.** Ninth and H'ers did what they do best – loitered, building memories – but only for the near-future, due to short-term memory loss.

6:20 p.m. A traveler's idea of a good time may differ from yours, and certainly varies from community standards – he got an early start on his party weekend by, police say, driving drunk, driving with an open container, possession of marijuana while motoring and driving on a suspended license. Next, an express flight from Dirt Merchant Central to the Pink House, courtesy APD Airlines.

• **March 20, 2001 2:16 - 2:32 a.m.** Some things are legal to smoke, but you have to be old enough. Others are illegal, unless you have a Dr. Feelgood license, which will setcha back a couple c-notes. That's the way it works right now.

• **March 23, 2001 12:35 p.m.** A lip-smackin' grown-up beverage glugged at Ninth and H bore a bitter, paperwork-flavored aftertaste for a local woman.

• **June 30, 2001 5:08 p.m.** Their brainpans basting in fermented distillates, two travelers at Eighth and F streets were arrested, booked and lodged in Big Pink, which stopped spinning after a while.

• **August 23, 2001 12:36 2:01 a.m.** Studies indicate that the mind-sharpening effects of marijuana and alcohol have the reverse effect on motorists, who crash and die a lot following their ingestion. Unless, that is, the imbibers are lucky enough to be arrested, as was this suspect in the 1300 block of 11th Street.

• **August 17, 2001 1:57 a.m.** This being a respectable Plaza social establishment, it's difficult to see what social progress you're going to make three minutes before closing time, so make like a tree.

2:15 a.m. A local man was arrested in the 1300 block of K Street on charges of exhaling putrid cocktail breath on a moving steering wheel, having already had a judge somewhere nullify his prestige with the DMV and refusing to accept the reality of locking steel loops about his wrists. Dennis' Dungeon engulfed another houseguest.

• October 30, 2001 2:55 p.m.

A passerby espied a glow
Inside of Apt. 16's window
And there, upon that verdant sill
Some flower pots all dressed to thrill
With modern meds, the leafy Kind
That dull the nerves and fog the mind
Cannabinators, four in number
Long on nugs and low in lumber
Two cops paid a cordial call
Saw the plants and on the wall
Above the THC-laced Soma
A Dr. Tod-endorsed diploma
Law and exigency gelled
Prop 215's umbrella held
"Thanks for your time," said APD,
"Good day." With that, they let him be.

• November 4, 2001 2:50 a.m.

A drinking man's friends went to war
Blocked driving his car to death's door
He stalked away shouting
But lived through the outing
And friends, that's what real friends are for.

Photo by Terrence McNally

Arcata, California, 2003.

Home Sweet Home

· **November 26, 1994 6:05 a.m.** Police received a report of a motorcyclist riding up and down Lewis Avenue yelling and punching a window on a parked car. A McKinleyville man pulled over by officers said he was upset over marital problems and his wife not coming home.

· **December 30, 1995 8:46 a.m.** A 10th Street man observed someone huddled in the bushes next to his home. Police found a McKinleyville man who said he was avoiding his wife.

· **August 3, 1998 2:10 p.m.**
Two folks from back east
Argued loudly on F Street
In true New York style.

· **September 26, 1998 11:35 p.m.**
Outside a tavern
He-and-she unpleasantries
Befouled the night air.

• January 12, 1999 10:30 p.m.
Love
Turning to dust
Slowly, publicly, painfully.

• January 16, 2000 12:15 a.m. They argued at McDonald's in the middle of the night. If they're lucky, this will describe the nadir of earthly existence for two area men.

• January 23, 2000 11:52 a.m. Love turned to embers, then ashes, but then flared with renewed heat when an ex allegedly threatened the former object of his affections. She asked that police document the hostility.

• August 2, 2000 7:46 p.m. Scott and Shannon disagreed loudly on the Plaza. Police thought Scott schnockered, and took him to the Pink House to allow his kidneys a peaceful environment in which to work their cleansing magic.

• August 19, 2000 2:08 a.m. Perhaps the he-she combatants along Tavern Row were battling over the secret formula or stolen microchip that will save the universe, or maybe they were just bitching each other out for lack of anything else to do. Police engineered a geographical solution.

• August 24, 2000 1:19 a.m. The delicate fluorescent ambiance of a 24-hour doughnut shop was either shattered or enhanced, depending on your perspective, by a public he-she frisson. The feuding fussbudgets took their leave.

• September 6, 2000 10:33 a.m. Amid the natural splendor of the world-famous Marsh and Wildlife Sanctuary, Amber and Mike serenaded migratory waterfowl with loud accusations of character deficiency directed at one another.

• September 7, 2000 2:50 a.m. It falls on future historians to make the definitive determination: Was she, as he alleged, a f*%#&? b*%#&? Or, as she claimed, did their problems stem from the fact that he was a f*%#&? a*%#&? Police asked them to move their deliberations away from the front of a tavern.

3:05 a.m. The above-described f*%#&? a*%#& was reported bellowing at the skies from Ninth and K streets. Prismatic glinting of the intersection's streetlamp off the officer's shiny badge had a tranquilizing effect.

• **September 22, 2000 1:08 p.m.** These neighbors aren't getting along, and it's come down to accusations of laundry stealing.

• **January 11, 2001 2:26 a.m.** A man was reported not just screaming, but yelling too, in the lower three-digit area of H Street, which is doing its best to cultivate a kind of Barbary Coast feel. The alleged eruptoid cannily refused to answer his door.

• **February 16, 2001 6:27 a.m.** Love, once burning bright, turned to faint embers, then ashes and accusations of car stealing. Technically, it was registered to him. The car, that is.

• **March 22, 2001 8:48 p.m.** That Magna Carta of the Sim Life crowd – the restraining order – again looked like a viable option after a harsh public confrontation.

• **March 23, 2001 12:50 p.m.** It's tragic, really, to ponder what interstellar trance was punctured by having a Center Streeter have to spark up the old left hemisphere so as to deal with a blue-suited man, just when the music was getting real good.

1:22 p.m. The cosmic love-pulse vortex on Center Street was stanched by an even more all-powerful City warning notice.

• **July 16, 2001 12:59 a.m.** A carbon-based unit's neural network engaged silicon-based circuitry via an audio/video/tactile interface in the 1500 block of Stewart Avenue. As the wetware digitally manipulated the chip's program architecture, it entered a period of synaptic overdrive marked by involuntary physical and verbal expressions sufficient to annoy the living piss out of a neighbor, who phoned the fuzz. Attenuate, Pong-boy!

• **November 18, 2001 5:51 a.m.** No, their alarm clock didn't shriek in a woman's voice, "I can't breathe!" It was the neighbors, having a wake-up spat.

Camping & Travelers

• **November 10, 1995 9:10 a.m.** Two outdoorspersons making camp in the remote wilds of Trail No. 1 in Redwood Park received a uniformed guest, who inspired them to mosey.

12:04 p.m. Four travelers enjoying a noon-hour bonfire under the St. Louis Road overpass left the scene with a fresh understanding of trespass laws and fire permits.

• **January 15, 1996 8:09 a.m.**
A Redwood Park 14th Street site
Where a guest made a nest overnight
The Canadian gent
Who pitched a small tent
Moseyed on by the dawn's early light.

• **September 4, 1996 9:54 p.m.** Two men were seen brawling on the Plaza. A witness walking home from the City Council meeting described the scene: "There were about six cop cars out there. A teenager had gone up to one of the 'hovel-grovelers' and said, 'This is my town, you hippie!'" Fisticuffs ensued until police broke it up and the disputatious duo departed. Hovel grovelers? "We call 'em 'hovey groveys,'" said the witness.

· August 20, 1998 7:57 a.m.
Oregonians
Redwood Park camping, were warned
Plus one in the car.

· October 1, 1998 8:55 a.m. Perhaps exhausted after saying "Intermodal Transit Facility," a man laid down on a bench and went to sleep, only to arise and roam away prior to police arrival.

· October 3, 1998 7:48 a.m.
Sean, Nicole, Jamie,
Camping here in Redwood Park
Is against the law.

· May 13, 1999 2:36 - 4:07 a.m. An officer roved around town, courteously jarring awake numerous campers whose I'll-sleep-here-unnoticed plans went awry.

· June 24, 1999 1:40 a.m. Hobo Junction, the freeway-side eucalyptus patch at 13th and F streets where a traveler's dreams soar on fumes of diesel exhaust, hosted three no-budget lodgers. They were warned.

· July 23, 1999 8:57 p.m. Rhonda from Modesto, Richard from Sunnyvale, Sandra from San Jose and Jason from New Hampshire enjoyed hearty – some would say boisterous, still others jackassian – conversation at their campsite in the primeval wilds between Safeway and the freeway. An officer greeted them with fresh information about the Arcata Municipal Code's opinion of urban camping.

· October 12, 1999 10:08 p.m. A traveler chose to make camp in the urine-saturated wilderness behind Tavern Row, and was warned.

- **December 22, 1999 12:23 p.m.** Two new mini-Ewok Villages were found not far from Trail 3. One of the camps was in the Arcata Community Forest, another in the McDowell property. Residents were told to pack up and leave.

- **January 7, 2000 10:10 p.m.** He attracted police attention by camping on the 14th Street side of Redwood Park, then was found to have an outstanding warrant. Off to that big, stupid-lookin' Pink jail they got down there.

- **March 2, 2000 5:46 a.m.** Perhaps he fancied himself a modern-day Marco Polo, trekking fearlessly to remote climes to witness hitherto undiscovered wonders. Or maybe the traveler just needed a place to sack out, and the entrance to the Chinese restaurant on 18th Street was dry. In any case, the far-flung foyer foray flopped, and the fellow was forwarded to the Pink House on old warrants.

- **May 11, 2000 1:18 a.m.** The modern equivalent of finding a fly in your soup – discovering a traveler in your yard – was the subject of a call-in from a Bayside Road resident. An addressless man was lodged in the Pink House.

- **May 24, 2000 5:30 p.m.** Three bush-dwellers near an F Street corporate pizza business were asked not to infest the shrubbery.

- **June 12, 2000 5:50 a.m.** Dawn's rosy fingers gave away the hidey-hole of a traveling man illegally camping at the Marsh.

- **June 19, 2000 10:01 a.m.** Sometimes folks get the bright idea of turning a mini-storage unit into a clandestine residence. Ray and Melissa were awakened on South G Street.

- **July 28, 2000 10:42 p.m.**
Perhaps they were rooting for grubs
Those gentlemen under the shrubs
The bushmen, sequestered
Were soon police-pestered
Away from J Street slumped the schlubs.

• August 2, 2000 3:20 a.m.
Tamara the traveler bunked down
On Transient Facility grounds
The illegal camper
Found slumberings hampered
When cops said, "Don't do this in town."

7:58 a.m. Three travelers pitched camp in a parking lot midway between Ninth and H and the Service Center, but soon found their idyllic lodgings invaded by an APD ranger. One outdoorsman allegedly lied to police, and was jailed.

• August 21, 2000 3:05 a.m. Good morning, sweet dum-dums. Guess what? The locals don't much like campers sleeping and depositing wastes in their premier park, where their children play amid your urine fumes, empty forty bottles and roaches. That being the case, wouldja get the hell outta here?

• August 24, 2000 4:15 - 8:16 a.m. Campers. Lots of 'em. All over the place.

• September 7, 2000 8:02 a.m. Picture the dank ramp down to the Udo Ut. Now imagine the damp coarseness of the cement against your skin. This was the best one camper could do for lodgings. A warning was delivered.

• September 8, 2000 3:13 p.m. Stark sunlight warmed the exposed nape of a traveler, slumped chin-to-chest in classic alk-stupe mode in the back of an APD cruiser on the way to the Pink House via the alley behind Tavern Row.

• October 8, 2000 6:05 a.m. The chirping of birds. The rustling of scurrying squirrels. The pit-a-pat of passing joggers. The rapping of a nightstick on the mandala-emblazoned window of your groovy van. These are the sounds which greet the illegal camper in the early morning hours in and around Redwood Park.

• October 10, 2000 5:58 a.m. No time for even a nominal wake 'n' bake for James the Redwood Park camper.

• **October 14, 2000 10:23 p.m.** Ryan the traveler popped the top on a refreshing adult beverage on the Plaza and took a hearty quaff. This fortification served to steady his hand as signed the citation.

• **October 18, 2000 5:20 - 5:50 a.m.** Two Redwood Park campers and their inevitable colonic gifts were prematurely awakened and cited.

• **October 23, 2000 9:01 p.m.** Motivational speakers Jason and Stephen made camp in a van down by the river, er, bus station. An officer warned them.

• **October 30, 2000 10:17 a.m.** Me cop; you camper. Outta Redwood Park.

• **November 4, 2000 9:39 p.m.** A bus camper may have thought the 1100 block of Fifth Street would offer sufficient obscurity to secure succor and guarantee a night of peaceful repose, but no.

• **May 25, 2001 7:11 p.m.** A traveler's stroke of sub-genius involved camping in a Fifth Street storage space. He was cop-toddled.

A more or less typical illegal campsite in Arcata.

Photo by Terrence McNally

Critters

• **July 5, 1994 9:50 a.m.** Someone complained about a rooster crowing in the 1300 block of Grant Avenue. The owner agreed to attempt to quell the cacophonous cock.

• **December 16, 1994 2:50 p.m.** An Anderson Lane resident heard footsteps on the outside deck of her home. An officer inspected the grounds, finding "fresh dog prints" on the deck. Animal activity; case closed.

• **January 15, 1995 10:30 a.m.** A dog chased a duck on Old Arcata Road near Golf Course Road.

• **April 11, 1995 7:40 p.m.** Juveniles were reported throwing rocks at the cows in a pasture in the 1600 block of 27th Street. The bovine bombardiers had boogied when police arrived.

• **May 7, 1995 1:37 p.m.** When a man came in asking for $50 for an African gray parrot valued at $1,000, a quick-thinking pet shop employee bought the bird and immediately phoned police while the seller hurriedly drove off. A "be on the lookout" bulletin was issued for the man over possible theft of the animal, but he was not found.

Shortly thereafter, Arcata Pet owner Don Bradner recognized the parrot as Malawi, a "very sweet bird" he had sold in 1988 and which had been stolen from an Arcata porch about three years ago.

Parrot and rightful owner were soon reunited.

"The bird was obviously happy to see him," said Bradner, adding that it was worth the 50 bucks.

"We were hoping for a Lassie-like ending," said employee George Scott.

• **May 11, 1995 11:26 a.m.** A man in the 1700 block of Old Arcata Road apparently attached shrubbery to his dog's collar as a deterrent after the dog dug it up, but other than potential embarrassment, no abuse to the animal was noted.

• **August 3, 1995 8:45 a.m.** A re-roofing project atop Gist Hall ground to a halt when a sparrow's nest was discovered in the path of the repair effort. Plant Operations officials contacted the campus Wildlife Management department, which sent specialists who identified the nest as that of a Nighthawk, a member of the Goatsucker family. "They're fairly common," said Dr. Rick Golightly, professor of wildlife management. The sole baby chick was removed to the Humboldt Wildlife Care Center, the mother flew off and work resumed at the site. "Mom will probably be back at the same place next year," said Golightly.

• **November 22, 1995 11:35 a.m.** The woman at the Post Office had neither license nor leash for her dog, and was awarded a citation for the achievement.

• **December 4, 1995 12:25 a.m.** A sick stray cat stuck in a heating duct was out of reach and out of luck. A cop on patrol couldn't pull it from the hole; the case was referred to Animal Control.

3:15 p.m. A gang of four sheep was seen swaggering around in the roadway on Spear Avenue west of Alliance Road. Community Service forces were dispatched, but the stealth mutton had slipped away.

Late Report The cat's still stuck, said a resident, way down inside the heating vent. Though Animal Control was sent, when they had came, the cat had went.

• **December 14, 1995 11:20 p.m.** A dog owner complained of people shooting at his pet while he was trying to call it in from running wild in a Janes Road field. He asked that the field's owners be told to call him before shooting at the dog, but the information was declined. Harassment of their cattle, geese and ducks by loose dogs from neighboring residences occurs too frequently to identify each dog and track down the owners, according to the six-year rangeland residents. "We'd be running a dog kennel here," said one.

Countless incidents of harassment and livestock losses over the years, including many documented in recent Police Log columns, have forced a policy of simply shooting the rampaging dogs, according to the ranger. "We lost a goose last night," he told *The Beacon* Saturday. "This is 'agricultural exclusive' property. If a dog's running your cattle or going after you it can be disposed of and should be disposed of."

The dogs enter the man's field through a barbed wire fence and through holes in a block-long wooden fence that were created by the recent storm. The rancher acknowledged while the dogs were "only playing... just having a ball," the ensuing livestock depredation was serious, and the fault of pets' thoughtless owners.

The man pinned the pet vs. livestock problem on Arcata's mix of Wild West traditions and contemporary influences. "It's a rural frontier western town, but with a college," he said.

The dog's owner could not be reached for comment.

• **December 15, 1995 9:01 a.m.** Another dog at play went after chickens in Myrtle Court, killing two before the resident intervened after hearing her own dogs sound the invasion alert.

"I heard the dogs and went out," said the chickens' owner. "He had finished one and had the other one by the back," she said. Animal Control was called and promptly captured the German shepherd, which was then taken to the Humane Society.

The dog's owner, a contrite college student, later reclaimed his pet from Humane Society kennels for a reported $40 and offered the chickens' owners $20 for their losses.

The chickens get along famously with the resident's own dogs, she said, adding that "they even sleep with them in the doghouse." The strange bedfellows are probably due to marauding raccoons, which killed 23 chickens in the past year.

"The 'coons don't bother our dogs," said the woman. "The chickens feel safer with them."

• January 2, 1996 2:27 p.m.
Loose brown dogs, a pair of them, marauding about town
Caused citizens to ask police to try to track them down
Arcata's only Animal Control has three weekdays
To round up beasts who frolic its bucolic back byways
A mahogany-hued mongrel romping Iverson and Q
Had scrammed, evading capture as a hound is bound to do
While out on Spear, another Chestnut cur had folks concerned
It too had gone, and where it went, police have never learned.

• January 16, 1996 10:34 p.m. A Villa Way resident asked for police assistance with her dog, which was having a frenzy in the back yard and wouldn't come to her. "He was barking and barking and barking and keeping the neighbors awake," said the owner.

Rudy the cocker spaniel's inspiration was a gopher in the throes of death after a yard encounter with the family felines, C.C. and Peewee. Rudy had been bitten by the gopher the previous week and was apparently celebrating. "The dog remembered it, I guess," the owner said.

An officer arrived and carried Rudy into the house, allowing the gopher to crawl off and expire.

"He's a nice dog," said Rudy's owner. "He doesn't bite."

• January 22, 1996 12:59 a.m. It was a dark and stormy night out at the plant on Ericson Way. The mill that manufactures clothes was closed up for the day. When sensors stirred, alarms went off, police soon found the cause – "Stripes" the factory cat had come inside to dry his paws.

• **January 27, 1996 9:30 a.m.** A Shirley Boulevard man working in his workshop was suddenly presented with a dead ferret by his two Golden retrievers. The resident was unsure what the "big, long, beautiful animal" was at first, until his wife, a Natural Resources major at Humboldt State University, identified it. Ferrets are fragile and ill-adapted to Humboldt's stormy clime, and the animal, a probable escaped pet, appeared to have died of exposure, said the resident.

A game warden with the state's Fish and Game department told police the man could dispose of the deceased beast himself, and he did. "That was a heckuva way to start the morning," the resident said.

Ferret-related calls come in "all the time," said Game Warden Nick Albert, since a large number of the cuddly, two- to three-pound weasels apparently reside secretly in Arcata-area homes. "A lot come in with college students, as pets," Albert said.

Though legal in 47 states, ferrets are banned in Massachusetts, Hawaii and California. Nonetheless, ferret accessories are readily available at local pet stores, and ferret fanciers hope to reverse the creature's legal status in the state via lobbying efforts and education campaigns. California's furtive ferret population has been estimated at up to 500,000.

• **April 14, 1996 4:36 a.m.**
A lone howling Hauser Court hound
Was car-bound, its human not found
A note left with Rover
Made Owner call over
He'd removed the dog and hence, the sound.

• **April 22, 1996 5:52 a.m.** The dogs begin baying at 3 a.m. at 11th and B streets. "I put up with it for a while, till my wife said it was bothering her, too," said a sleepless citizen. "It just kept up and up and up, like they were after something." Concerned that the caterwauling canines might be "hung up" or in some jeopardy, the man called police.

An officer arrived and one of the dogs dutifully trotted over to him, with the other one soon to follow. The raccoon – the object of their vocal affections – took swift advantage of the opportunity to escape the tiresome affair, clambering down the tree and bounding off. Nearby Campbell Creek is a popular commute artery for prowling raccoons out on their nightly rounds, according to the neighbor.

• **May 23, 1997 3 p.m.** If you were a loose dog in a world of asphalt and right angles, you'd hang out at the fragrant bagel shop, too.

• **June 3, 1997 5:15 a.m.** A yap-happy pooch in the back of a truck was positioned behind a Plaza hotel, where it could share dogly concerns with sleepy lodgers.

• **September 28, 1997 3:12 p.m.** A clapped-out raccoon staggered up the 1600 block of Charles Avenue, alarming residents. An officer came out and dispatched the ailing beast to the choir invisible.

• **October 11, 1997 4:56 p.m.** A renegade cow was re-pasturized on Saratoga Way.

• **July 8, 1998 10:54 p.m.**
When security silently sounded
A vet clinic soon was surrounded
Police looked around
The alarm source was found
A hound, once impounded, which bounded.

• **July 9, 1998 9:25 p.m.** What fun it is to throw bones into your Alliance Road neighbor's yard and watch his dogs fight.

• **August 29, 1998 4:56 p.m.**
On 10th Street near Q
Five trespassers and their dogs
Endured a lecture.

· September 1, 1998 1:15 p.m.
Two peacocks got loose
Flounced on Zehndner Avenue
Then back to the pen.

· October 3, 1998 7:49 p.m. That yappy dog was taken inside.

· October 6, 1998 10:02 a.m. Damn peacocks.

· November 6, 1998 4:30 p.m.
Iverson and Q
A lone cow wandered the streets
Not for very long.

· November 22, 1998 2:27 p.m.
On F, by the store
A tied-down dog nipped someone
The owner was warned.

· February 11, 1999 9:15 a.m. A deceased cow was spotted in a Samoa Boulevard field.

1:45 p.m. A different dead cow was seen in a South G Street field.

· February 19, 1999 9:40 p.m. A tangled drama of little lasting consequence played itself out when an injured dog, a black lab, was reported at Dirt Merchant Central. The pooch was located at about the same time another report came in from a nearby resident, who said his dog had been attacked by a black lab. A man came to pick up the black lab, and by that time the man whose dog had been attacked wasn't answering his phone, so a message was left on his answering machine. It falls to future historians to reconstruct the matter from that point.

· July 10, 1999 Late Report A big dog was found running loose and unable to explain its past, and was taken to the Sequoia Humane Society.

• **August 14, 1999 12:18 p.m.** Some who have studied canine behavior assert that dogs have the most intense emotional life of all mammals. So why tie this sensitive creature down in a truck at Ninth and I streets?

• **August 15, 1999 9:45 a.m.** Described by the owner as "the most beautiful chicken I ever knew," this particular poultry, a 10th Street resident, was "a little bit different than the others." Known as "Clucky," the favored fowl soon burst into song, to the annoyance of neighbors. It was then that the feathered one's human overlord realized Clucky was actually a rooster. Since chances of obtaining a Conditional Use Permit for a gender dysphoric boy-chicken are questionable, the caterwauling cock was given away.

• **August 25, 1999 10:05 a.m.** Police took two loose dogs into custody in Redwood Park. The owner, nowhere around as her unleashed pets romped and shat freely in the picnic zone, was notified by answering machine.

• **August 29, 1999 2:46 p.m.**
More dogs on the loose, Redwood Park
Free to run, chase, growl, fight, crap and bark
Way out of control
Until cops on patrol
Pointed out to their irresponsible owners the large-lettered signs all around which clearly read, "Dogs must be on leash."

• **October 8, 1999 2:49 p.m.** Three ducks were reported walking in the roadway on Bayside Road between Union Street and Crescent Way. Tripod, the three-legged alpha duck, likes to ramble, but his extra leg gets caught up in the others, immobilizing him and his wacky-quacky entourage. An Animal Control officer returned all to their owner.

• **October 12, 1999 12:01 a.m.** A resident in the 1500 block of Old Arcata Road reported loud animal screams in the field across from her home. Police found only serenity.

• **October 27, 1999 1:12 p.m.** Tripod, the misunderstood three-legged alpha duck, led his charges on a wacky-quacky quixotic quest down Bayside Road, alarming motorists. The ambling adventurers were gone when police arrived.

• **November 12, 1999 5:12 a.m.** After a barking dog complaint on Chester Avenue, an officer hung out there for 10 minutes, detecting a singular arf. The matter was forwarded to Animal Control.

• **November 17, 1999 1 p.m.** After numerous complaints of domestic ducks running loose in the roadway in the 200 block of Bayside Road, a resident was issued a second warning notice and a copy of the relevant Arcata Municipal Code regulation for future reference.

• **January 5, 2000 2:45 p.m.** A loose goat reported at Spear Avenue and West End Road eluded detection. This is the creature whose double-wide pupils take in all the human comedy pursuant to roundabout confusion.

• **February 22, 2000 6:06 p.m.** Another case of welcome to my unrestrained dog. Three oblivious Redwood Park users were warned.

• **February 26, 2000 9:52 a.m.** A cow made a break for it on 11th Street, but was swiftly rounded up.

• **March 11, 2000 1:45 p.m.** Loose dogs roamed Redwood Park, charging people, running through picnics and shitting in the children's play area as their humans gazed on adoringly. Police warned several owners.

• **March 13, 2000 7:55 a.m.** A dog ran loose around an I Street Mexican bagel shop, no doubt near-crazed by the aroma of fresh-baked handouts.

2:30 p.m. An overly aggressive domestic goose was found at the Arcata Marsh and Wildlife Sanctuary. It was taken to the Humane Society.

• **March 22, 2000 4:43 p.m.** A loose cow was reported on

Alliance Road near Westwood Court, but on officer arrival was neither seen nor herd.

• **March 29, 2000 6:06 p.m.** A raccoon at the end of its autumnal years was transferred from Union Street to the Corpse Yard.

• **May 9, 2000 1:10 a.m.** A woman spotted some guy in her Union Street backyard. A man was trying to free his dog, which had become entangled in berry brambles.

Late Report Still another dog stuck in berry vines on Union Street. What are the odds?

• **May 23, 2000 10:23 a.m.** A truck swang into a handicapped parking spot at Redwood Park and disgorged its load of a half-dozen canine travelers, creating instant "dog chaos." Police were called, but arrived only after the pets had voided their innards onto the lawn and playground area.

• **May 30, 2000 3:34 p.m.** A dog-human strolling unit at the Marsh were warned that they should be linked by an umbilicus.

• **June 14, 2000 6:47 p.m.** Loose horses sauntered proudly down Janes Road. The steeds arrived at a Heindon Road address, where the resident, who was acquainted with the owners, made arrangements with same for the animals' return.

• **July 3, 2000 8:48 p.m.** The Sunny Brae bear made a cameo on Beverly Way.

• **July 14, 2000 9:30 p.m.** Two loose dogs attacked another dog near the Spear Avenue/West End Road roundabout. The two-pooch pack was returned to a nearby yard, and a note left, which the dogs, try as they might, could not read.

• **July 21, 2000 4:50 p.m.** Maya the traveler looked on adoringly as her dog shat on the Plaza grass. A nearby business employee called police, who advised the dog owner of the complaint. She cleaned up the poop.

• **July 24, 2000 4:40 p.m.** A horse enjoyed a brief release from human domination at 17th and Q streets. Then they fixed the fence.

• **August 5, 2000 3:36 a.m.** Police were called to arf-rich Ribeiro Lane to deal with chronically barking dogs.

• **August 7, 2000 3:35 a.m.** A loose horse in Valley West was corralled.

• **September 8, 2000 1:38 p.m.** Cows made it out of their pasture onto Bayside Cutoff, but proved too stupid to take their liberation from enslavement any further.

• **September 19, 2000 3:50 p.m.** Dog chaos engulfed the 14th Street side of Redwood Park. An officer contacted several pooch owners, who waited for him to go away so they could re-release their super excrete-o-matics in the picnic area.

4:20 p.m. Human and canine idlers accreted to the limits of physical density at the Ninth and H Nug Exchange Mart, reaching critical mass and achieving a certain banal irony, owing to the particular witching hour. Any ambient poodles or other dogly denizens had been promptly stashed on the moment of police arrival.

• **September 29, 2000 9:10 p.m.** A cow rampaged on Vassaide and V streets.

9:11 p.m. The bovine race launched a probe – consisting of a volunteer among its ranks – into the human-dominated world beyond the sodden pasture upon which it is confined. The subservient species reabsorbed its hero, all involved having probably forgotten the whole point of the excursion in favor of chewing on muddy grass.

• **October 16, 2000 9:28 a.m.** Dogs ran happily amok on the 14th Street side of the Redwood Park Fecal Coliform Farm.

• **October 24, 2000 10:22 p.m.** A J Street dog tangled in its tether set up a whining misery sentinel which had little effect on the owner's roommate, but did prompt a complaint from an adjacent J Street resident. Police talked to the roommate, who promised to disentangle the pretzeled pooch.

• **November 5, 2000 8:40 a.m.** An altogether too-friendly raccoon wandered from patron to patron at a car wash at 10th and K streets. Fearing that its normal raccoon inscrutability ethic had been compromised by rabies, the clearly impaired beast was transported to eternal peace via shotgun.

• **December 27, 2000 3:20 p.m.** A woman apparently believed that connecting her foot with her dog at high velocity in an I Street parking lot would impart wisdom and obedience to the unsatisfactory creature. Both were gone when police arrived.

• **January 11, 2001 2:11 p.m.** Her heart leapt with joy as her dog, her companion, her friend ran free through the Humboldt State University campus. Others did not share in the delight. Police returned her dog, her companion, her friend, her menace, and offered cordial disillusionment.

• **January 17, 2001 3:48 p.m.** A manchild and his dog reportedly argued in the 1400 block of G Street.

• **January 19, 2001 Late Report** Dogs waited for their two-legged alpha, adorably guarding the driver's seat, but prompting concern for their well being. The two looked OK, and a note was left for their human.

• **January 30, 2001 Late Report** Brazen bovines made a break for it on Samoa Boulevard, but were re-enslaved forthwith.

• **February 15, 2001 1:15 a.m.** A dog secured and exposed to the elements in the open back of a pickup truck in the 1100 block of 12th Street whined pitifully until a neighbor notified police, who took it into custody and left a note for the loving master.

• **March 8, 2001 5:03 a.m.** A rooster dutifully cock-a-doodle-dooed on Redwood Avenue. Well, it was morning.

• **March 12, 2001 2:33 a.m.** A loose dog scampered about Sunset Avenue, triggering envious arfs from yardbound dogs in the area. Information was forwarded to Animal Control.

• **March 13, 2001 11:34 a.m.** Frenzied dogs penned inside a vehicle as the owner blithely gallivanted about town exploded with rage with each passerby, who experienced a momentary loss of dignity with their fright reaction. Animal Control left a "nice nasty" note.

12:36 p.m. The guy who has more or less homesteaded the corner of 17th and G streets and runs the daily dog-and-sign show there was asked not to utilize the entire sidewalk for same.

• **June 3, 2001 5:15 a.m.** A yap-happy pooch in the back of a truck was positioned behind a Plaza hotel, where it could share its dogly concerns with sleepy lodgers.

• **July 22, 2001 10:01 p.m.** A deer was struck by a vehicle and critically injured in the 1700 block of Old Arcata Road. It was dragged out of the roadway and, in its best interests, had its brains blown out.

• **August 28, 2001 9:03 p.m.** How that boa constrictor got from one upper G Street apartment to another one's oven is not immediately apparent. The serpent was repatriated.

• **September 15, 2001 12:47 p.m.** The county Health Department has put the North Coast Growers Association on notice that dogs will not be tolerated in a food market – a little problem with produce glistening with dog pee – and the City has tried to keep the weekly community festival alive by stepping up Plaza patrols. A woman brought her dog to the Farmers' Market concealed it in a bag, reasoning that since it wasn't down "on" the Plaza but held in an enclosure, it was OK. Ah, but since the dog law doesn't include the phrase "except in bags," and, alerted to the situation by someone who'd still like to attend the Farmers' Market a year from now, police issued the dog owner a highly-resented ticket.

"Orick Johnny" Antonioli, 1921–2003.

Photo by Kevin L. Hoover

Characters

• **April 20, 1994 7:05 p.m.** An elderly man was reported lying in the grass in the 200 block of I Street. Johnny told police he was just resting and needed no assistance.

• **November 15, 1994 9:50 a.m.** An H Street beauty salon complained of someone acting weird outside the business. A man matching the description told officers he had been admiring the architecture of the Pythian Castle.

• **February 6, 1995 11 a.m.** An Arcata man came to the station to report an assault by a suspect known only as "Frog." The alleged amphibian attacker had left the area when officers arrived.

• **May 12, 1995 2:19 a.m.** An officer observed a "transient" man camping in the 600 block of F Street and warned him against camping within City limits. "I was sleeping under a church," said Pete. "I was real sick and I fell asleep." Of his brush with the law,

Pete said, "He was a nice person. I went on my way and he went on his way."

• **July 5, 1995 7:42 p.m.** A report came in of a slumped figure at a Giuntoli Lane bus stop. Pete had fallen asleep.

• **July 6, 1995 7:08 p.m.** An anonymous caller asked that police check out a guy in a wheelchair at 11th and K streets who was hitchhiking and almost falling over. Marty often does this, and it makes everyone nervous, especially when he rolls his chair backwards up the middle of the street and cars are swerving around him. It's always a bad situation, but in this case, the D.A.R.E. car came to the rescue and a friend was found who could take him home.

• **October 26, 1995 11:33 p.m.** Pete suffered a broken rib and bruised eye at Spear Avenue and Alliance Road after late-night martial arts horseplay with an associate got out of hand. "We was just playing, and before I know, he hit me," said Pete after spending the night in the hospital. "I'm a little bit weak, but I'll be all right," said the well-known local street person. A possible suspect was identified. "The Lord said we're supposed to love our enemies," Pete noted.

• **November 29, 1995 9:59 a.m.** A concerned citizen reported a traveling man described only as "Rags" urinating in public in the 1000 block of H Street. The suspect couldn't be found, and the complainant declined to pursue charges.

• **February 5, 1996 6:21 p.m.**
A dumpster in far Valley West
Reportedly hosted a guest
Who dove in the funk
To plunder its junk
Till flushed from the trash treasure chest.

• **April 22, 1996 8:49 p.m.** Pete and Frank were thought to be vandalizing a bus stop in the 2500 block of Alliance Road, but were in fact just enjoying a spirited sojourn at the stop with no evidence of criminal activity.

• **May 15, 1996 3:05 p.m.** Just 23 hours later and three blocks north of the previous day's incident, gridlock again visited G Street when rainy day antics of two men clogged traffic and held employees of a bank spellbound. "I pulled into my bank parking lot and this guy came up to my car," a patron recalled. "He asked for a light for his cigarette." But seeing that the cigarette was drenched with rain, the patron dismissed the favor as flagrantly farcical.

When ignition was denied, the man migrated his quixotic quest for fire to the nearby intersection. To the amusement of a blanket-clad companion giggling nearby, the sodden smoker went from car to car pretending to ask for a light, impudently walking in exaggerated slow-motion as cars backed up down the block. "Every car that would come up, they would hassle them," said a witness. "They were standing in the middle of the pouring rain, stopping traffic. It looked like they had nothing better to do."

Inside, bank personnel gravitated toward the front of the business to better follow the action. "The whole bank was watching, pretending to work while they looked out the window. I was watching, too," said the patron. The performers then caught sight of their captive audience and one employee reportedly turned away in embarrassment, saying, "We got caught."

Timing is everything in vaudeville, and whether by fate, signal or instinct, the street jesters suddenly abandoned their performance and ambled off toward the Plaza, missing by moments the arrival of police. "They were definitely very entertaining, kind of annoying," was the capsule review of one witness.

• **June 20, 1996 2:03 p.m.** A man who had reportedly been directed to a private bathroom in a Plaza building found the door locked, and chose a corner of the hallway about 15 feet away to relieve himself. The leaky fellow was quite literally collared – uplifted by the scruff of his shirt – by a businessman in mid-zip, and when police arrived the traveler was cited. An employee noted that restrooms are available to the public at the Intermodal Transit Facility (bus station) at Ninth and F streets.

• **July 5, 1998 5:42 p.m.** A business reported a suspicious subject clad in blankets shambling aimlessly in the 1400 block of

H Street, gibbering affectionately at passing women and meekly asking others for coin kibble as he clutched at his ragged hobo habiliments. Pete the media superstar was just doing his very own Pete thing; no crime.

7:46 p.m. A citizen reported someone lying in the footpath at Stewart Court. The reclining Ragman was savoring his beer buzz, and wandered off.

• **July 19, 1998 10:26 a.m.** An H Street business reported a suspicious man with a disturbing crew cut and ponytail coiffure frequenting the business.

• **November 16, 1998 4:48 p.m.** Police performed a Pete-ectomy at a Northtown laundromat. The Ragman was jailed on a trespass charge.

• **February 28, 1999 7:43 p.m.** The Pirate and some pals were driven from the ever-popular carport in the 800 block of Ninth Street.

• **April 21, 1999 2:29 p.m.** Marty and the Pirate elaborated on their latest philosophical divergence outside a Plaza liquor store.

• **July 14, 1999 10:32 a.m.** The Pirate, back from his Maui sojourn, received the latest addition to his collection of citations for camping in Redwood Park and outstanding warrants.

• **August 31, 1999 8 a.m.** A fussbudget without portfolio was asked to leave a California Avenue market.

8:58 a.m. Another man vs. fussbudget encounter on Laurel Avenue. Fussy was told not to contact man unless absolutely nec.

10:49 a.m. Some obstinate spare changers interfered with pastry digestion outside a Plaza bakery.

3:57 p.m. Some mouthy dingbat hung with Marty outside the Post Office for a while, annoying passersby with intrusive banter. Both were warned about disturbing the peace.

5:25 p.m. Dingbat was warned about disturbing innocent villagers at Eighth and H streets.

6:31 p.m. Dingbat got hisself ejected from a brightly lit F Street supermarket.

• **October 2, 1999 4:45 p.m.** The Pirate's preferred afternoon summer refresher, Gallo Tawny Port, again fueled a mission to the Pink House.

• **October 22, 1999 3:11 p.m.** After a camping complaint, an officer found a bunch of the Pirate's stuff stashed in blackberry bushes on South F Street. It was taken to the police station and later picked up by the kindly buccaneer without portfolio.

• **November 9, 1999 10:52 a.m.** A woman's car bumper reportedly bumped Marty's wheelchair ever so slightly.

• **November 24, 1999 6:23 p.m.** Moe, allegedly from Earth, became Moe from the Pink House after being arrested on a warrant near the Plaza.

• **November 28, 1999 4:15 a.m.** Pete conked in the donut shoppe. With prompting, he awoke and shambled away.

2:40 p.m. Pete appeared not to comprehend the go-away message that a Northtown coffee house was sending. More shambling.

3 p.m. The further adventures of Pete, now discomfiting taco consumers at a nearby fast foodery. Away he went.

• **December 15, 1999 4:21 p.m.** Pete stood dazed in the roadway at 14th and H as cars whizzed past him at uncomfortably close range. A brief negotiation ended with the Ragman agreeing to stay out of the roadway.

• **January 3, 2000 5:02 p.m.** Johnny thought a car near his house was parked illegally, but it wasn't.

• **February 16, 2000 10:52 p.m.** Marty was marooned, asleep in his wheelchair in the bike lane in the 1100 block of K Street. His dad came and got him.

• **February 18, 2000 9:01 p.m.** Marty was reported making a disturbance in the alley behind Tavern Row. Now he's not welcome at one of the bars anymore.

• **June 8, 2000 12:33 p.m.** Pete isn't supposed to be drunk in public, both due to his probationary status and in the interests of his health. But he was, so he and his motley blanket scraps were gathered up and deposited in the Pink House.

• **June 30, 2000 5:21 p.m.** If he had been, say, 12 or 13 and out goofing with friends, it might be understandable. But this guy was 18 and flying solo as he went pee up and down the stairwell and in the elevator in a downtown office building just as people arrived for dinner at the popular restaurants there. The whiz kid was caught in the act upstairs and the chase was on. Down the stairs, out the back door and around the building he ran, with security guard Gary Wallace in pursuit. As the two reached Eighth and H streets, the 46-year-old nabbed the 18-year-old, and marched him back inside to face the music and pee. Police soon arrived, but the property owner chose not to press charges, so the kid got off with a warning – and cleaning up all the wee-wee splattered everywhere. All the excitement took place on Wallace's last day on the job.

• **August 27, 2000 Noon** Had they been equipped with a handy spray-can of *Weirdo Begone*, the Plaza business might have doused... no, drenched the place with it. Instead, they called police.

• **October 11, 2000 1:37 p.m.** Slithy toves gyred and gimbled in the Ninth and H wabe, and it wasn't even brillig. Larry looks good in uniform, and made the desired impression.

3:20 p.m. Borogoves and mome raths numbering perhaps 20 held an impromptu soiree at Ninth and H streets. Another APD niceguy wielded charisma, and the walkway clottage dissolved.

• **October 12, 2000 6 p.m.** A suspected Bandersnatch was confronted by a backpack-theft victim at Ninth and H, and some discussion ensued. A positive identification of the backpack proved frumious, and an offer to return it was declined.

• **October 13, 2000 3:57 p.m.** The chainlink fence at Ninth and H seemed as comfy as a Tumtum tree to a zoologically uncategorizable assortment of manxome toves. An APD Jabberwock came whiffling through the tulgey wood, mome raths galumphing in mere anticipation of his burblings.

5:40 p.m. Lewis Carroll's rotational velocity notwithstanding, gimbling toves with borogoves on a hemp leash burbled about Ninth and H. An APD officer's smile, like a vorpal blade, dispersed the uffish oafage.

8:52 p.m. A group of rowdy, possibly mimsy toves amassed outside the newly-refurbished entrance to an I Street cooperative supermarket.

The Pirate, L. Scott Rebman, with his buddy, Marty Spier.

Photo by Kevin L. Hoover

- **October 15, 2000 2:58 p.m.** More toves gimbled, loitered, dumped refuse and knocked back bevs at the Intermodal Transient Facility. A beamish boy in blue broke up the parking lot party.

4:05 - 5:58 p.m. Odds are the toves arrested at Ninth and H on charges of public frabjousness were less than tulgey as the cuffs went snicker-snack behind their backs.

- **October 24, 2000 7:34 p.m.** Pete was reported banging on a door and yelling at a Northtown apartment building. Something about money. The Ragman was mincing from the scene when police arrived.

- **January 22, 2001 5:25 p.m.** Alan told Pete he could sleep around the back of the house, it's OK.

- **February 16, 2001 9:55 p.m.** A trailer world resident was reported banging on the walls of his real good deal-o. Subsequent investigation revealed that the subject sports a mullet-style hairdo.

- **March 21, 2001 5:17 a.m.** There must be five Petes, since the Ragman is frequently spotted in Valley West, Sunny Brae, Northtown, Four Corners, downtown and elsewhere seemingly simultaneously. This time, he was ambulanced from the Marsh Interpretive Center to the hospital for treatment of cuts after taking a fall.

7:56 a.m. Pete, having received treatment, took a sojourn at Janes and Upper Bay roads, but a passing kindergarten teacher became concerned for the ragged, bandaged figure slouched on the corner. An officer found Pete just being Pete, albeit on the Bottoms.

- **August 30, 2001 6:35 p.m.** Is Pete still alive? It's not an infrequent question, and as of this date, the beloved Ragman was giggling it up with a newfound best friend on the railroad tracks behind the K Street mini-storage complex. The happy couple shuffled on down the tracks.

7:04 p.m. A woman was reported waving her hands and singing at Eighth and K streets. Police found no sign of her, or her likely muse Pete for that matter.

• **October 8, 2001 12:55 a.m.** Out for a midnight howl, a Center Street man profaned the cosmos, then retreated to his lair, mission accomplished.

1:02 a.m. Two more "transient-looking" representatives of the hairier gender, with their even hairier four-legged friends, were observed in a dispute with a third guy wearing short hair and a red plaid shirt. The longhairs supposedly whapped the other fellow with a skateboard, but his plaid armour apparently helped him withstand the impact, because when police arrived, no one was there.

• **October 10, 2001 10:39 p.m.** Powerful currents of alcohol-laced beverages coursing through his mullet-capped brainstem, a trailer park resident equipped with a stick and chain enjoyed his First Amendment right to free expression, but neighbors didn't, and the term "shrieking inanely" appears nowhere in the Constitution. His muddled furies – but not the arcane apparatus – were contained within the Pink House.

• **November 13, 2001 2:15 p.m.** A sneaky-lookin' white guy with a big-ass Afro 'do... well, that alone. But this one-weirdo experiment in multivultural perversity had also been seen lurking near an unoccupied house on J Street, arousing suspicion. Somehow, the large-haired subject eluded detection.

• **November 16, 2001 1:05 p.m.**
A man at the front counter said
An antenna'd been placed in his head
Is it yours? he asked cops
And with that, wandered off
To get back, one would hope, on his meds.

• **November 18, 2001 10:44 a.m.** A guy mowing the lawn on the grounds of an outer Eighth Street vehicle rack manufacturing concern got an earful above and beyond the drone of his machine. A rugged individualist who lives a block away took issue with the mowing, citing the "early morning hour." Police advised him to go to his room. Big mowers kept on mowin'.

Arcata's beloved "Ragman," Pete Villarreal.

Photo by Kevin L. Hoover

Musicians

• **April 25, 1994 5:45 p.m.** A man was reported playing drums loudly inside his van. A traveling man agreed to curtail the activity.

• **July 7, 1994 11:16 p.m.** An F Street resident complained of people playing drums in a laundromat parking lot. The drummers were gone when police arrived.

• **February 23, 1995 9:55 p.m.** Officials at a social club just off the Plaza asked for assistance with managing a large crowd teeming at their front door in anticipation of a "grunge style" rock music presentation. Officers assisted in clearing the entrance alcove, sidewalk and street.

• **May 19, 1995 12:04 a.m.** Roiling, bongo-based reverberation engulfed the Redwood Bowl. Officers sought the source of the disorderly conduct in the bowl and adjacent areas, but all was quiet and the midnight percussionists escaped justice.

· October 20, 1995 12:04 a.m.
On the Plaza, percussory pests
Threatened slumbers of close hotel guests
The bongos were silenced
With reason, not violence
Allowing tired lodgers their rest.

· October 23, 1995 9:13 p.m. Another in the time-honored tradition of after-hours drummers on the Plaza agreed to stop.

· October 26, 1995 1:39 a.m. Still more bongos on the Plaza met with the usual result.

· November 8, 1995 6:14 p.m. Police went to an F Street carport where someone was heard yelling. Five people had taken shelter from the rain there and subsequently burst into song. Advised of the bad review, they agreed to quiet down.

· November 11, 1995 2:49 a.m.
As bongos boomed on through the morn
The hotel got police on the horn
This is buggin', they crowed
Till an officer showed
On the square, quiet calm was reborn.

3:16 p.m. A fed-up neighbor complained about a daylong music and drum fest on Blakeslee Avenue. A warning notice deployed at ground zero wet-blanketed the unfortunate affair.

· November 18, 1995 12:56 a.m. The rooftop of a car parked in the 900 block of J Street apparently proved an ideal venue for a man to hold forth at some length on a pair of bongos. An unappreciative resident phoned police, who related the complaint to the perching percussionist. Soon quiet was restored. Bongos, an Afro-Cuban instrument, originated in the island nation about 1900 and have vaulted to local prominence as the most commonly used serenading utensil for Arcata's downtown.

• **November 24, 1995 8:17 p.m.** A woman complained of loud drums in the 800 block of Bayside Road. The drummer said he had already arranged with the woman to be contacted if he was too loud, and that he would be completing his percussory endeavors soon.

• **January 2, 1996 4:40 p.m.**
The thrumming of drums bummed someone
Who summoned police to the square
Officers urged the sonic scourge
To move their act elsewhere.

• **February 2, 1996 10:50 p.m.** In the first reported eruption of bongo fury within Arcata city limits in 1996 (though, if history serves, not the last), a Zelia Court resident complained of pounding percussion throbbing up the intersection of Alliance Road and Spear Avenue. The bongo stylist, a nearby resident, agreed to keep the noise down.

• **February 5, 1996 8:12 p.m.** A 10th Street woman was watching a movie in her home when "very loud" drumming began resonating through the neighborhood.

A conga pilot was holding forth from a car wash stall across the way, and though the woman tried hard to ignore the pernicious pounding, her patience eventually wore down and she phoned police. "I like music. I'm not complaining about that," she said. "But two hours? Come on." The woman said that between the car wash concerts and another noisy neighbor, she was moving, and soon.

"It echoes out," said the musician, who utilizes the acoustically sumptuous stalls from time to time. He said car wash patrons and passing street musicians appreciate his work, often joining in the musical merriment with instruments at hand.

Pursuant to the nearby resident's complaint, an officer arrived at the car wash. There, policemen and percussionist agreed that that night's program of practice was complete.

• February 17, 1996 2:42 a.m.
In the air one early morning
Drums provoked a noise report
Loudly pounding sounds aborning
Thrumming up from Tilley Court
Police arrived, one man recalled
Tempered the percussion quest
Asking "Just calm down"
The ill-timed bongo fest was laid to rest.

• February 22, 1996 11:36 a.m. With bongo tensions in town running at fever pitch in the wake of anti-noise legislation introduced the previous night by a unanimous City Council vote, a concerned citizen called in a complaint of numerous persons playing the diminutive drums at residential flats in the 1000 block of 10th Street. The bruited bongo barrage was actually a rehearsal of Mazel Ala Shi Mazel, a two-man klezmer music band consisting of a clarinetist and a doumbeck player. "We are audible," acknowledged one of the musicians, "but I think we were pretty melodic, too. We actually play good music."

The Klezmorim combo had been readying themselves for a scheduled performance that night at a multimedia "Ritual Transcendental Transubstantiation" event at Celebration Hall, to benefit Free Arcata Radio, the town's pirate radio station. The band and significant others had been rehearsing out in the front yard of the ramshackle dwelling when they apparently alarmed the citizenry, but had retreated to an upstairs apartment by the time police arrived. There, they were advised of the noise complaint and things were quiet when police descended down the dank, urine-scented staircase.

A resident expressed that the responding officer had placed his foot in the doorway while speaking to apartment occupants. The officer said later that keeping subjects in view was key in that type of situation. "It's a safety concern," he said. "If you're talking to somebody and they shut the door, they could be going to get a weapon."

A band member blamed the new anti-noise measure, enacted but not yet in effect, for the bongo brouhaha. "I've probably played a hundred times since I've lived here and this is the first time the cops have come," he said. "I think it relates to the noise ordinance."

Some 12 hours later, an L Street resident complained of loud music blaring from the Celebration Hall benefit. As police arrived, volume levels at the transcendental ritual were already plummeting as raver attendees transubstantiated into homebound pedestrians. In the end, about $160 was raised for the quasi-legal radio station.

• **March 13, 1996 3:55 p.m.**
From the town's grassy square rose a rollicking rumble
Percussion commotion made Plaza peace crumble
A policeman appeared, took the pulse of the street
And four drummers there beat a hasty retreat.

6:57 p.m. Three hours later the drummers resurfaced
Rattling passerby, making some nervous
Police then returned to the square for a sounding
Persuading the people to postpone their pounding.

7:35 p.m. Despite all the warnings they'd heeded before
The foul flagellators were flailing once more
One last time the officer went to the site
The bongo squad hung up their skins for the night.

• **June 28, 1996 1:12 a.m.** The zip of a noise complaint warning notice being ripped from a ticket book unsuccessfully battled a booming stereo for the attentions of partygoers at an L.K. Wood Boulevard apartment.

• **June 9, 1998 11:18 p.m.** The Ninth and H Street Percussion Ensemble erupted with rhythmic expression for a brief time.

• **June 30, 1998 9:52 a.m.**
In the 1000 block of H Street
Percussionists, less than discreet
Erupted in song
But before very long
A cop stopped the bongo-borne beat.

• July 30, 1998 4:56 p.m.
At Ninth and H streets
A concerned citizen saw
young minstrels in song.

• September 13, 1998 7:52 p.m.
The zone around Parkland and Mack
Was where a loud bongo attack
Erupted and ended
So when cops descended
They left with no need to come back.

• September 15, 1998 9:45 p.m.
That unstoppable bongo beat
Again bubbled up on I Street
The kioskville clumpers
Included some thumpers
Who then chose to be more discreet.

• September 21, 1998 10:44 p.m.
Bongosity once again surged
And kioskville drowned in the dirge
Of late-night percussion
But after discussion
The drum-bonking throng purged their urge.

• March 9, 1999 4:56 p.m. Early signs of spring aborning
include longer days, budding flowers and the ephemeral percussive
majesty of bongos filling the air in the 1000 block of G Street. The
artist was advised of the complaint.

• March 10, 1999 12:28 p.m. A Ninth and H-er's hand drum
artistry overwhelmed a nearby businessperson with reverse
admiration. The percussion victim asked that police reduce
the thumpage quotient, and soon the sonic backdrop was again
dominated by the musical rumble and roar of internal combustion
engines.

• April 20, 1999 2:28 a.m. A street minstrel in the 800 block of
Ninth Street was asked to stop his godawful guitaristics.

- **May 20, 1999 8:39 a.m.** Them infernal bongos erupted at Ninth and H, but the menace was gone on police arrival.

- **July 17, 1999 2:56 p.m.** Bongo pilots throttled up at Ninth and I streets.

9:07 p.m. Plaza percussorators completed their drumming chores for the night, to the relief of a nearby resident.

- **July 19, 1999 6:19 p.m.** Two bongo pilots who had alighted on the Plaza were warned not to dilute the sweet music of roaring auto exhausts all around with their percussive squalor.

- **July 22, 1999 7:06 p.m.** Bongo horror bathed kioskville on I Street. A rhythmic group was briefed on official Ecotopian percussion policy.

- **August 12, 1999 5:49 p.m.** A bongo crisis at Ninth and H dissipated before government forces arrived.

10:38 p.m. More bongo horror at Ninth and H streets. A traveler packed up the portable percussion and continued his journey through the cosmos.

- **August 14, 1999 2:12 a.m.** A Long Beach party host reveled in boisterous SoCal style up on Sunset Avenue, drawing Arcata Police. A neighbor shuddered in horror as she recalled the ultra-annoying tune the party's rock band was playing: "When Johnny Comes Marching Home." Whether due to their abominable choice of repertoire or the holes in the walls which they had festooned with drained beer bottles, the rockin' rebel residents were shortly evicted.

- **August 29, 1999 2:38 a.m.** As taverngoers whooped it up and cars, trucks and motorcycles roared all around, it was a lone djembe player (as usual, misreported as a bongo stylist) that received government attention on the Plaza. He discussed the odd, selective nature of noise complaints with an officer, who took the percussionist's points but nonetheless was compelled to enforce the Arcata Municipal Code, which, in Title 4, Chapter 3, Article 3,

Section 4335, Part B, states:

"It is unlawful for any person to use any musical instrument or device of any kind in any public space or right-of-way within the Downtown Plaza area for any cumulative period exceeding fifteen minutes within a twenty-four hour period. This section shall not apply to any person who has been duly authorized to engage in such conduct by the granting of a variance by the noise control officer pursuant to Section 4360 of this Chapter."

• **September 3, 1999 12:43 a.m.** Plaza bongo pilots offered skull-throttling artistry to unwilling hotel lodgers, prompting a complaint. They were gone on arrival.

3:09 a.m. More bongosity. A bonker was warned.

• **September 13, 1999 9:33 p.m.** The recessed doorway of a Plaza shoe shop offers a handy, sometimes urine-soaked amphitheater for footloose minstrels, their fans and their bodily by-products. Too many and the cops come.

A bongo pilot (actually, that's a djembe) on the Plaza.

Photo by Kevin L. Hoover

· September 21, 1999 2:27 a.m.
When bongo magicians at play
Erupt on the Plaza each day
Well, some of the time
We set it to rhyme
'Cause Emily likes it that way.

· September 28, 1999 2:35 p.m. A bonk-and-run bongoist briefly threatened municipal tranquility, then moved along.

· September 29, 1999 1:52 p.m. Another bongo atrocity on the Plaza. But the suspects quickly lost interest, perhaps distracted by a bright shiny object.

5:34 p.m. As bongo interpreters thumped
A clerk at a Plaza store grumped
A cop soon responded
He nodded, they bonded
The dinnertime drum din was dumped.

· October 2, 1999 1:25 p.m.
Two bongoists, throttling same
Set Plaza percussion aflame
Police pulled up short
And made them abort
Their 15 scant minutes of fame.

· October 4, 1999 1:45 p.m. Bongo fury, southside Schwazz.

· October 25, 1999 1:55 a.m. Bongo magic enlivened/degraded the quality of life in the 800 block of Ninth Street.

· October 30, 1999 3:03 p.m. Merciless percussionists were reported torturing a bongo on the Plaza. Its anguished cries had subsided when the government arrived.

· November 23, 1999 3:35 a.m. A guitar-equipped caterwauling carport caroler was poorly reviewed by a sleepless upstairs resident, who summoned police to the Ninth Street location.

• **February 18, 2000 1:52 a.m.** A saxophone stylist was asked not to blow his horn on the Plaza for more than 15 minutes. That's the law, as stated in the Arcata Municipal Code.

• **May 22, 2000 10:06 p.m.** There's something about 10 p.m. that so says, "stop playing drums."

• **July 19, 2000 9:12 p.m.**
At Ninth and I streets, bongo bopping
Kept sidewalk enthusiasts hopping
Transacting in nugs
The sitabout slugs
Bonked on till a cop counseled stopping.

• **July 22, 2000 5:22 p.m.** Daniel and Robert, master bongoists, broadcast a beat over the Plaza. They were soon visited by City mojo-harshing specialists.

• **August 8, 2000 8:08 p.m.** Despite a local mayor's hopeful and oft-repeated boast that the Age of Bongos has passed, the accursed/beloved instrument again rang forth from Ninth and H, inducing bliss and headaches, depending on one's temperament. The bongo pilots were advised.

• **August 17, 2000 9:33 p.m.** Bongo merriment proved short-lived on the Plaza.

• **August 20, 2000 6 p.m.** Again the Ninth Street resident found his cerebral cortex resonating involuntarily to the primal thrum of a bongo-like instrument being utilized at Ninth and H. An Oregon man chilled with the bonkage.

• **September 2, 2000 3:35 a.m.** A South J Streeter must have been suffused with the sheer joy of life or something to be shrieking while sharing his rock-style music with the neighborhood at near-seismic volume levels. Mr. Exuberance next found himself nodding solemnly at a policeman who was standing in his doorway.

• **September 8, 2000 8:53 p.m.** Only another drummer can know how much fun this guy was having along Tavern Row.

9:09 p.m. The little drummer schlub didn't want to lose the supreme vibe, so, in the interests of continuity, he scuttled over to Ninth and G for more percussive squatting. And yet, the hotel complained.

• **September 13, 2000 10:07 p.m.** On Wisteria Way, more thundering minstrels yielded to the sounds of silence.

• **September 21, 2000 6:21 p.m.** Grotzman Road only seems like the country. Despite its rough-hewn road surface, it is in fact suburban Arcata, where a rockin' teenage combo may hone their furies only at peril of a noise complaint.

• **September 29, 2000 9:35 p.m.** This music's so righteous, everyone in the neighborhood's gonna want to hear it!

• **November 19, 2000 5:22 p.m.** A non-drummer can never understand how having to play more quietly inevitably changes the experience for the worse.

• **December 26, 2000 4:11 p.m.** That drummer on Stromberg must be getting pretty good, what with the five-hour practice sessions and all.

• **January 22, 2001 3:29 p.m.** The sound of that bongo was like a searing needle plunged into the cerebellum of a Plaza businessperson. The artist ceased his bonking and left.

• **March 8, 2001 7:07 p.m.** Bongo fury at Ninth and H? Dude, that's so two years ago.

• **August 16, 2001 7:57 p.m.** Those enjoying the exquisite dialogue, pacing and all-around artistry of a Shakespeare play in Redwood Park were distracted by a more contemporary, low bit-rate form of amusement involving repetitive, trance-inducing bonking of hand drums, often accompanied by joyfully prancing and defecating dogs. Two counterculture groups were asked to allow the more traditional fare to proceed uninterrupted, and did.

• **September 19, 2001 10:17 p.m.** Turn it down! I have children sleeping here! Don't you boys know any nice songs? (On Stromberg Avenue.)

• **October 22, 2001 6:17 p.m.**
He thought that he would never hear
A sound so ugly in his ear
A drum whose thrumming pulse is wrought
Upon the Redwood Park north lot
The beat that thunders forth all day
As fuzzies chug their nugs and bray
And strip the trees of branches, bare
To burn in barbecue pits there
Upon whose soggy, turd-lined plain
Loose dogs deposit stench and stain
Drums are bonked by dudes like these
But only cops can gain surcease.

• **November 17, 2001 6:06 p.m.** Avant garde musicians at – where else? – Ninth and H streets experimented with a new guitar technique which involved using a person's head as a plectrum against which the instrument is slammed like a cudgel, creating the inimitable and exotic El Kabong tuning.

Guitar Dan.

*Photo by
Kevin L. Hoover*

Slices of Life

• **November 13, 1995 4 p.m.** A man observed wandering around the Blue Lake School turned out to be a U.S. Marine on leave, just "remembering the old times."

• **February 16, 1996 12:49 a.m.** Heralding the new day, an Eastern Avenue man vibed on his porch, drinking wine and enjoying some Grateful Dead tunes. Waves of the aural flux washed over a neighbor who was on a different plane of consciousness, harshing her lifestyle. She then reported the harmonic misconvergence. Soon, police arrived and restored tranquility anew to the zone with a timely realignment of energy levels. "I just turned it down," said the man.

• **February 25, 1996 12:04 p.m.** A man drove up to a Valley West paint and hardware store in a new, shiny black pickup truck and roamed the store, then left without making a purchase. On his way out the man lifted the lid from a plastic trash can out in front of the business, threw it in the bed of the truck and drove off.

"I think I figured it out," said an employee. "I'm pretty sure he wanted to use it as a snowboard." The appalled employee said customers had been clamoring for the boards all day, but that the truck driver was the first to score a lid instead. "It's flat-out incredible," the employee said. "He can pay $15,000 for a truck but he can't go buy a snowboard."

• **April 3, 1996 12:50 p.m.** As neighborhood residents looked on, a tough-talking teenage boy smashed a bottle on the sidewalk in what may have been a bold effort to impress some barefoot girls nearby. The neighbors promptly went over and asked the youths to clean up the spray of glass shards, offering a broom and dustpan for the task.

"What business is it of yours?" countered the recalcitrant bottle breaker and several surly cohorts, voicing additional unsolicited character insights regarding the gentleman who was offering the janitorial hardware (who later acknowledged that some of the accusations had foundation, but were irrelevant and certainly no excuse for creating a public hazard).

The crabby crew then withdrew, so the man and his wife went over and swept up the two-dimensional plume of glass shrapnel themselves. "It's our neighborhood. It's incumbent on us to do it," said the man.

"Puberty does strange things," he reflected.

• **April 25, 1996 9:03 p.m.**
A witness described a dark vision
Of vehicles in a collision
Police went and checked it
Found two cars connected
Assuming the jump-start position.

• **May 9, 1996 6:19 p.m.** Some of the patchouli-soaked nomads who spend their days in the parking lot at an I Street cooperative supermarket get downright surly when asked not to block the thoroughfare and disrupt business. After reminding one pet owner of dog ordinances, an employee got a face full of threats. The menacing mutt master was gone when police arrived.

• **May 14, 1996 4:09 p.m.** A white "grammar school conversion" bus trundled east on Eighth Street past the Plaza, then attempted to turn right into the oncoming one-way traffic of G Street. The dreadlocked driver apparently had other things on his mind and had grossly miscalculated the vehicle's turn trajectory. As its front left wheel came to rest against the opposite curb of G Street, the bus lurched to a stop two-thirds of the way through the turn. With the arcing ark jammed at an angle across the busy intersection, northbound cars became mired along its starboard flank and traffic backed up down the street past the gas station.

Observers say the pilot of the landlocked landship responded with a twofold crisis management strategy, which involved loudly comparing blocked G Street motorists to the final stage of a digestive tract while simultaneously flailing at his stickshift in search of reverse. The grating, gravelly graunch of grinding gears gave coarse counterpoint to the caustic chorus of curses.

"It was kind of unusual to see a guy try to make a right-hand turn onto a one-way street using three lanes, and there aren't three lanes," recalled a witness.

Eventually, the monster motorhome backed out of the intersection, then roared up onto the sidewalk of G Street and parked, listing forward on the downhill incline and still facing the wrong way as pent-up traffic "shot by" in a petulant frenzy. With slackjawed passersby gazing on in the aftermath, the driver bounded from the bus over to a brown Ford Torino waiting across the street and "made some kind of a buy," according to an observer. Back at the bus, the driver had cracked open a can of beer and was brazenly guzzling for all, including arriving police, to see.

A traveler was subsequently arrested on suspicion of public intoxication and probation violation, then lodged in County Jail. A traveling woman was cited for possession of marijuana, then released.

"Why didn't they just write 'Bust Me' in red paint on the side of their bus?" wondered one citizen.

• May 17, 1996 2:31 a.m.
On H Street, a voice in the night
Yelled loudly to "Come out and fight!"
The warrior wailed
Then up and turned tail
Before finding someone to smite.

· June 4, 1996 6:39 p.m.
An I Street cooperative store
Had guests that it could not ignore,
Though frequently fingered
The travelers who lingered
Had worn out their welcome once more.

· June 30, 1996 8:37 a.m. An upset fellow with lots to say wandered into a business, found a sympathetic ear and went off on a nonstop monologue that began as the lamentation of a broken man and escalated into a raging rant.

"Nobody understands," the man began, sagging against a counter and weeping. From there the diatribe became increasingly bizarre. "He said he'd been dead and he'd come back from Hell and that he was Satan," said the employee. "He said he was going to raise his children from the dead, and that if his blood was put in sick people it would heal them."

The rhetoric grew more scrambled and the man became increasingly aggressive as he "rambled on for over an hour," according to the employee. Eventually, the man got right in the employee's face with his harangue and she retreated from the verbal onslaught. "I kept backing up to the back door," said the employee. At the right moment, she said, "I was going to run out the back."

Just when the woman became cornered at the rear of the business, an opportunity came and she seized the moment. When other customers suddenly entered the area, the man glanced away and she ran into the back room, locked the door and called police. "The cavalry came," she said. "While I was on the phone talking to them the police were here, also sheriffs."

The man continued to fulminate as he was "wrestled into a police car," according to the employee. "He saw my Bible and said he hated Christians and women, and I'm both," she said. "He said, 'I have to get angry for my heart to slow down.'" At his request, the man was given a ride to the Eureka Rescue Mission.

· June 11, 1998 3:03 p.m. There's this guy, see, who has some kind of imaginary beef with the cooperative folks over at the former Purity supermarket on I Street. The fellow's outrage over who-knows-what culminated in his wailing incoherently at a baffled employee at the customer service window, then grabbing the telephone and flinging it in a petulant frenzy.

The tiny but torrid tirade of terror continued as Mr. Testosterone went out around the side of the store and bashed in some windows, then scampered. Police tracked him down, cited him for public drunkenness, vandalism and obstruction of a police investigation and carted him off to jail. Employees were left to deal with the broken glass and crumpled window screens.

• July 22, 1998 1:58 a.m.
Fifth Street, 500 block
A plaintive cry, beckoning
Where are you, my friend?

• October 21, 1998 3:51 p.m.
On witnessing Eric's tattoos
Jeff, Aaron and Charles were amused
They taunted and teased
Till found by police
And admonished for verbal abuse.

• November 17, 1998 4:45 p.m.
On S Street a 12-year-old cried
And a spanking was swiftly applied
Though the corporal measure
Caused someone displeasure
The tantrum was soon to subside.

• November 19, 1998 1:29 p.m. A traveler chose the front
area of an H Street antiquarian bookstore to articulate, at high volume and to no one in particular, his lengthy, profanity-laden list of complaints against the cosmos. Police shared quality time with the chap.

• December 6, 1998 5:25 p.m.
Skate punks at the high school swarmed
Requests that they leave met with scorn
Police came to see
That the quad was skate free
Young rollers nearby were then warned.

• **January 2, 1999 5:24 a.m.** A fellow obviously whacked on multiple chems tried to spend serious money – in the upper four figures – at a Plaza business. But though his credit was good, the ethical retailer decided that the pieplate-pupiled customer's judgment was not. She wouldn't let him blow his money, so he left, and the staff put everything back. Later, the sobered-up big spender expressed appreciation for the shopkeeper's uncommon valor in protecting him against his excessive tendencies.

• **January 14, 1999 11:51 p.m.** A nice old lady zoomed out of an optometrist's parking lot in Sunny Brae and whamsmacked a passing car to the tune of $1,200. "I didn't see you," the lady said to her accidental target. Relish the irony.

• **February 11, 1999 9:56 a.m.** A restraining order's conceptual force field wasn't powerful enough to deter an alleged violator from getting too near, and he went to jail.

• **March 5, 1999 1:14 p.m.** Let's see, Eighth and F streets, that's just one block away from a fully functional public restroom. Ah, but why expend the effort to trudge over there when all the world's your pissoir? A leaky chap was warned.

• **August 31, 1999 8:09 a.m.** A fired motel employee didn't take it well, making a scene in the parking lot. An officer stood by as he gathered his possessions and took his matchbook-cover career in motel management elsewhere.

• **September 2, 1999 7:37 a.m.** When things don't work out, it's always the children who suffer.

• **September 29, 1999 8:26 p.m.** Dude, it's over with her. No calls; no visits.

• **October 5, 1999 8:12 a.m.** Why should a hard-working person have to look out their office window and see some guy peeing in the bushes at a South G Street public park? A traveling man was warned about the quality-of-life impacts of his actions on innocent glancers-by.

• **November 1, 1999 5:41 p.m.** Someone was reported beating on a vehicle in the parking lot of a 13th Street marketplace. It was just a dad trying to wake up his four year old. Late naps, as many parents learn the hard way, are highly problematic.

• **November 2, 1999 10:43 p.m.** At 17th and H streets she sat, weeping. Where could her dog be?

• **June 24, 2000 12:35 - 1:51 a.m.** Let's just skip the tawdry details and say that tavern patrons utilized every last chance to get drunk and stupid prior to closing time, sodden sleep, a thundering hangover and a scraggly lawn you've put off mowing for two weeks, honey.

• **August 16, 2000 1:40 a.m.** It began with the violent slide-bang-rattle of an elderly VW bus' side door opening. The rickety clatter of the open louvered windows finally subsided to the cooing sounds of man and animal reuniting. "Hoodoo? Hoodoo? Here boy..." queried the drunken voice. "Good boy." The clunk of a plastic bowl on the sidewalk, followed by a pointillistic crescendo of kibble descending into the bowl and spilling onto surrounding cement. "*Gooood* boy..."

Next on scene were two fellow travelers – one with what sounded like a severe bronchial infection – exchanging hail-fellow-well-mets in appropriately booming tones which resonated nicely off of nearby buildings. Hoodoo, by this time, had dutifully lightened his bowl, which *skritched* noisily across the sidewalk as he plumbed its last morsels.

And for the next hour, the human/dog mobile party unit used the listing white V-dub van as a jolly-time base camp complete with doors slamming, sounds of unknown fluids streaming, rip-roaring oaths and curses, kibbitzing, joking and toking. The one sick-sounding guy uncontrollably coughed and spat at an alarming rate as Hoodoo happily prowled and utilized area yards to dogly ends. The affair more or less settled down around 3 a.m., with Hoodoo and company all somehow bunked down in the little tilty hippie van.

When police finally arrived about 4:15 a.m., the goodtime solipsists were well and truly zonked, with officers' rapping on the window only serving to reawaken nearby neighbors as the objects of official attention pursued much-needed coma therapy. Their inquiries ignored, the officers went away, allowing the celebrants to more or less rewrite the Arcata Municipal Code there and then to allow camping within City limits.

The next morning, a sleep-deprived neighbor went out and opened the van's side door, causing a human head to dazedly arise from a swirl of blankets inside. Police were soon back on the scene, this time less inclined to be ignored. When it became apparent that officers weren't just going to give up and go away, the battered microbus' sliding side door opened halfway and the alpha zonkling then tumbled from the van along with Hoodoo's filthy plastic dish, which immediately became wedged 'neath the listing van and the curb.

Unforgiving morning sunshine burned starkly down on the squinting party boy, harshing his well-earned torpor. He was soon presented with a camping citation which he initially refused to even remove his hands from his pockets to sign. An officer then explained that what he was being asked to sign was only a promise to appear and not an admission of guilt, and that if he didn't sign it he would be immediately taken before a judge for a hearing on the matter. Since the fine young gentleman was hardly dressed for court, he reluctantly scribbled his name and was handed a copy of the ticket. "Have a fuckin' great day," he said as he snatched the ticket from the officer's hand, though his tone of voice seemed to imply that he wasn't really concerned with the officer's well-being at all.

An embarrassingly bright orange derelict-vehicle sticker was then slapped on the windshield, but the crapvan remained in place for another day or two. It then disappeared, leaving behind only a pool of motor oil destined for the stormwater drain leading to Jolly Giant Creek, a broken window roll-down handle and the lingering stench of urine. Hoodoo could not be reached for comment.

• **October 14, 2000 11:51 p.m.** Hello, honey? I'm up in Arcata. No, not Arcadia – *Arcata*. Look, I'm in jail; some crap about driving drunk. Hey, can you wire the bail money up here? Honey? *Hello?*

• **October 28, 2000 1:19 a.m.** Hilltop Court residents awoke to a house-shuddering impact they at first took to be an earthquake or a tree fall. But a glance out the window revealed the cause to be a fellow who'd driven his truck at high speed directly into the house. Neighbors later reported having heard the truck accelerate with a squeal of tires at the mouth of the cul-de-sac as it sped toward the home.

As residents phoned police, the driver sat, apparently dazed, in his pickup truck/battering ram amid the ruins of the stairway, window, pipes and telephone wiring which had cushioned his impact. He then pulled backward and slowly drove away, trailing debris and timbers from the house, some of which were later recovered a mile away, but leaving the grille of the truck embedded in the house. A McKinleyville man was soon arrested at U.S. Highway 101 and State Route 299, and jailed on drunk driving charges. Next morning, he sheepishly appeared at the victims' home, offering insurance information, an apology and a lame explanation which left most questions unanswered: "I screwed up and got lost." The repair bill came in at $2,000.

• **Saturday, June 23 3:47 a.m.** Oxygen flow to their neocortical decisionmaking circuitry perhaps constricted by trans-fatty acid-drenched heart-attackian cuisine dispensed at a chain greasery in the 3500 block of Janes Road, several subjects became baboonishly boisterous. Then, in a maelstrom of hoots, hollers, slammed doors and narrowed arteries, they got in their hooliganmobile and roared away.

• **July 12, 2001 10:36 a.m.** I'll swear at the middle-aged woman bank teller, and that will make her want to help me. Somehow the plan backfired.

• **August 20, 2001 2:05 a.m.** Another "belligerent" ambassador from McKinleyville got as far as a 24-hour restaurant on the northernmost part of our cool town before attracting police attention. Read more about the ways of those they call McKinleyvillers in their native habitat in the *McKinleyville Press,* proud member of the Mad River Newspaper Guild, available at Arcata Liquors and by subscription. See *www.mckinleyvillepress.com.*

• **August 21, 2001 12:53 a.m.** The caricature of the drunk with a top hat swinging on a lamp post found a modern iteration in the party manimal glugging hooch, a spray of liquor globules clinging to his chin, the topography of his his grizzled rictus tattooed with a grid of chainlink shadow on the pedestrian footbridge.

11:20 a.m. An E Street multiservice center asked for help with a flagrant fusspot. The snitwit boogied.

• **August 29, 2001 8:39 a.m.** They think they know who it was that broke into an I Street business, spent the night and then showered before leaving without stealing anything.

• **August 29, 2001 9:41 a.m.** Someone entered a closed South Plaza building, helped themselves to some clothes from one shop and reggae supplies from another, then pooped in the hallway and left.

1:55 p.m. He was a classic – fuzzy of head, clad in rags, backpack and bedroll, squatting with dog-on-a-rope while smoking a ratty little rolly right outside a Plaza shop's front door, smiling and striving for gainful eye-contact with passing brothers and sisters. On making the acquaintance of a uniformed fellow human, he meekly took his leave.

• **Thursday, November 22, 2001 5:36 a.m.** A bakery worker shivered outside the business, waiting for a higher-ranking employee to open the place so he could start his shift.

6:49 p.m. A woman out walking in the Marsh as night fell encountered a man who rode up on a bike, greeted her and initiated small talk. Perfunctory preliminaries accomplished, he next asked if he could take her to dinner. She declined. He then scaled back the request to having coffee. Another no, and as she walked toward the all-too-distant City lights, Mr. No-Means-Maybe apparently figured he just hadn't selected the right form of social recreation and pressed his quarry to attend a movie with him. Again she rebuffed his clumsy courtship and asked him to leave her alone. The clod-on-wheels finally got the message and rode off.

Making her way to the South I Street parking lot, the woman noticed a dark, four-door hatchback circling, its lonely pilot formulating his next approach. As she walked up I Street towards home, he pulled up alongside and asked her out again, as though a desperate drive-by come-on might be the beginning of something beautiful. "Leave me alone!" she said, and ran way, but he began pulling his car around toward her. She fled. Again he got close and told her, "It's dark out here. You have a long way to go." Frightened, and in an effort to buy time, she humored him with small talk, and he sped off.

She soon encountered another man and asked him if he'd accompany her back to town, which he did. Eventually she reached the sanctuary of her home, only to find the Marsh stalker there and waiting, as though he had followed her. Apparently hoping to capitalize on his wealth of accumulated charisma, he introduced himself as "Jeff," and notified her that he was an Aquarius. Reverse-captivated by this sodden singles-bar datum, she called police, who checked the Marsh and environs but only found some other people who were told that the area is closed to the public after dark.

Jeff is described as having short black hair, baggy eyes, a dark complexion, wearing dark clothing and probably single.

• **November 26, 2001 11:30 a.m.** A dweller in a high-density residential inn on Union Street reported someone having thrown an object on her porch, consisting of several bottles plus medicine containers all taped together. The message being...?

• **November 27, 2001 3:48 a.m.** The person who had gifted his neighbor with taped bottles and pill containers was on the line, asking for an officer to visit him. He wanted off the continent and back home to Israel, he said. He'd found some opium from 1940, yet still suffered from a dislocated shoulder and blacked out, but against this adventuresome backdrop somehow managed to enjoy his first meal in 12 years. An officer went to the man's home and found him agitated. After calming down, the man agreed to go to his room for the night.

**Signs of varying
specificity and
urgency.**

*Photos by
Kevin L. Hoover*

Messages

• **March 3, 1994 11:05 a.m.** A clothing store in the 5000 block of Valley West Boulevard reported the theft of a sign reading "WE QUIT" off the front roof of their building.

• **August 29, 1995 4:38 p.m.** "Why is the music and art kept inside?" asked the chalk message near the Music building. "Free the books" demanded a similar chalk scrawl outside the Library. Unknown suspects.

• **September 27, 1995 3:30 a.m.** A stolen wallet was found and returned to UPD. Some $30 cash had been taken. A note found inside of the wallet said "Thanks."

• **November 20, 1995 2:10 p.m.** The word "KEG" was reported burned into the turf at the Redwood Bowl in six-foot-tall letters. Police determined that a weed-killing potion was used to emblazon the monosyllabic message.

• **December 1, 1995 12:06 a.m.** A marijuana leaf taped to an exit sign in Sunset Hall was removed and destroyed. No suspects.

• **February 7, 1996 9:50 p.m.** An apartment dweller in a residential area of town discovered an unsigned, typed note which had been left on her car. The writer apparently believed the vehicle belonged to a Humboldt State University student trying to scam some free parking at the complex. The note read, in part: "A parking permit is cheaper than a paint job. Don't test us."

The recipient of the letter took it to her landlord, who reportedly admitted having authorized another tenant writing it, but hadn't anticipated that the note would be vicious or threatening. The woman then wrote her own letter, explaining that she was a tenant and that any vandalism would be reported to the authorities. She attached copies of the original maladroit missive and her reasoned response on every door in the complex. "I didn't want to be immature, like them," she said.

The awareness campaign apparently worked, as parking peace has prevailed at the location ever since.

• **February 19, 1996 10:25 a.m.**
With "scruffy" beard, denim coat and pants
He strode up G Street, looking askance
At campaign signs there on display
And tore down two along the way
Then scampered, sans apology
No theme of ideology
Defined the scruffian's design
A witness said, "He was out of his mind."
On the Plaza, post-conniption
Cops stopped a soul of his description
Who fast denied the dirty tricks
Disclaiming hands-on politics.

• **July 18, 1998 8:32 p.m.** A man who goes around certain parts of town pulling illegally posted flyers down from utility poles extended his enforcement to a private home on I Street. The resident complained after the man removed from the side of his house flyers made from enlarged photocopies of newspaper items about the man taking down flyers. But, concerned about the proliferation of involuted conceptual vortices and their effect on the time-space continuum, the resident decided to conserve his energy. He then rescinded the complaint, but put up a new batch of clippings.

• **June 11, 1999 4:48 p.m.** Maybe he didn't see the "No" on the "No dogs" sign of the Plaza. Or maybe, unlike his pet, he didn't give a crap. Either way, a traveler was cited.

• **August 21, 1999 9:53 a.m.**
As farmers sold goods on the square
A man tried to pitch poems out there
He had no address
And found little success
At flogging his word-woven wares.

• **August 29, 1999 10:57 p.m.** The devil showed his hand on Alliance Road, and it held a black marking pen. Satanic drawings were scrawled on a bedroom window, indicating that business must be slow and free time in abundance for the once-proud Prince o' Darkness.

• **November 3, 1999 5:50 a.m.** Numerous small, independently owned businesses, along with the Post Office, the pedestrian footbridge and other apolitical edifices were graffitized by anti-World Trade Organization activists.

• **May 1, 2000 6:10 a.m.** Was it vengeance for the Exxon Valdez, or just random vandalism that motivated the damage to windows and gas pumps which occurred overnight at the gas station in the 1400 block of G Street?

• **June 28, 2001 10:09 a.m.** Stoner-age cave paintings uglied up a K Street mini-storage complex.

• **August 21, 2000 2:47 p.m.** Reports flooded in of a man

standing on the Plaza screaming. An officer found him just reading poetry in a loud manner, and didn't bother taking his name.

• **September 17, 2000 3:32 a.m.** There are those who climb mountains. Some write novels. Others strive to define the sublime physical forces which compose the universe. This guy's mark on civilization involved banging his tiny fist against the window of an Alliance Road stop 'n' rob. Police headlights flashed across his greasy handprints, but the overachiever had moved on to better things, which in this case would be almost anything.

• **September 30, 2000 1:12 a.m.** A squad of bike-borne vandals bashed the crap out of random objects with plastic bats as they passed through the area of Haeger Avenue and Austin Way. Perhaps, as some schools of thought hold, they were unempowered victims of a world gone mad expressing themselves as best they could in a desperate gambit to achieve personal validation and reaffirmation of selfhood. Or maybe they were just morons.

• **November 6, 2000 10:03 a.m.** As if the City could lay cement at 14th and K streets without it being inscribed for the ages with a personal message.

• **November 8, 2000 7:22 p.m.** A guy shared his confusion with the world, bellowing abstrusions while tapping on a hand drum as he marched down H Street.

• **January 27, 2001 1:19 a.m.** Direct Action – the humiliation of a Giuntoli Lane beverage vending machine – brought corporate America to its knees.

• **February 18, 2001 12:44 p.m.** Some young people write software that revolutionizes the music world. Others track comets and asteroids with self-made telescopes. And then there are the mouth-breathing Brainiac larvae who apply their discretionary time to trudging around in the dark, spray-painting various surfaces, such as sewage pumping stations on Old Arcata Road.

Food

• **November 21, 1994 4:10 p.m.** A report came in of a vehicle with spaghetti on it in the Creekview Apartments parking lot. Police investigation revealed the noodles to in fact be angel hair pasta.

• **July 22, 1995 12:55 a.m.** An officer noticed people dumping debris onto the City Hall parking lot. Two McKinleyville residents said that coffee grounds and rice had been slathered on their car while they were watching a ball game. They had to clean it up.

• **April 1, 1996 4:10 p.m.** Two men sat down at a G Street restaurant and ordered a late afternoon meal. One man ordered a chicken and ham sandwich with fries. The other fellow wanted a burrito and a beer, but since he had no I.D., the brew was refused. The pair were served, but after a while restaurant employees noticed their booth vacant but for dirty plates and a pair of wool socks left on the seat. "They took the ticket with them, too," said an employee. Police checked the area to no avail. Total loss $13.57. The socks were tossed.

• **March 17, 1999 5:43 p.m.** He looked like a "regular joe," the waiter later recalled, except for those haunting, "bulgy eyes." The guy ordered a barbecued beef on Dutch crunch and a Coke, enjoyed the healthful repast and boogied without paying. An officer checked the area around an historic Plaza storehouse, to no avail – the diner had dashed.

• **July 28, 1999 11:12 a.m.** A person was deemed of insufficient character to patronize a midtown by-the-slice shop.

• **August 8, 1999 4:50 p.m.** A dine 'n' dash at a Northtown Chinese restaurant.

• **August 23, 1999 1:26 p.m.** Thieves stole refreshing cola goodness off the back of an unguarded delivery truck in Valley West.

• **September 1, 1999 4:26 p.m.** As a Plaza eatery came to life in preparation for evening diners, grills were fired up, tables were set and the floor vacuumed. About this time, a Plazoid wandered in to use the pay phone in the hallway, but the whooshing floor cleaner made it rather too hard for him to concentrate on his conversation. Soon thereafter, a major BAM! and some subsidiary wham-bang-booms were heard by office workers on adjacent floors, who wondered what the...?

Evidently, the excitable fellow had become "perturbed" at the droning vacuum cleaner and did the only logical thing – bodily wrenched not just the pay phone, but the entire carved-oak phone frame from the wall. His sense of justice unsatisfied, the enraged conversationalist dragged the massive telephone assembly down the hallway with ripped wire entrails flopping along behind as he ineffectually hammered at the restaurant's walls and cut-glass windows with the plastic phone handset in a shrieking display of protest at the unfairness of the situation.

When he reached the Chef's Special sign a few feet away, matters took another ugly turn as the flimsy plexiglass holder advertising tantalizing Fresh Ahi topped with a piquant lime-butter sauce, served with rice pilaf and grilled pineapple slices, $14.95, was mercilessly sundered from its mount and left to languish on the floor.

With his conquest over pressure-molded plastic items demonstrated to a degree certain, the testosterone-charged soul then wandered down a passage fortunately bereft of punishable outcroppings, which led him to the street and a fresh start in life, one hopefully free of mean vacuum cleaners.

But, as employees looked on agog at the entertainment rampage, the raging rambler offered an innovative final flourish upon his exeunt – that of hurling an umbrella at a white-hatted kitchen assistant whose lettuce-chopping activity evidently linked him to the vacuum's cruel effrontery. And at that, he was gone, if not soon forgotten.

• **July 2, 2000 6:28 p.m.** Dazed millabouts teemed in slow motion at Ninth and H streets, some of them manifesting enough energy to throw food at each other in what may have been a non-verbal form of communication or ritualistic sociocultural activity.

• **January 13, 2001 2:23 a.m.** Deadbeat diners did a scarf 'n' scram at a Janes Road 24-hour restaurant.

• **February 16, 2001 4:14 p.m.** The term "defrauding an innkeeper" may evoke enchanting images of adventure and romance in medieval times – mammoth mutton legs washed down with grog from a pewter chalice; furtive rolls in the hay with a country maiden; swashbuckling escapes on horseback... but in this case, a Rio Deller allegedly scarfed down some deli fare and boogied from a 13th Street marketplace. She was cited, booked and released.

• **February 17, 2001 4:24 a.m.** After several youths were thwarted in their plan to sneak into a motel's pool, they sought succor and fries at a nearby fast food stand.

Town & Gown

• **February 21, 1995 10:30 p.m.** A custodian reported a combination of burning candles, pounding bongos and marijuana smoking in progress in the Field House. Two persons were cited for marijuana possession under one ounce, and two non-students were escorted off campus.

• **October 7, 1995 6:26 p.m.** A combined bongo/guitar outbreak near Pepperwood Hall drew officers. The suspects left the area.

• **December 2, 1995 1:29 a.m.** Three cars in the Jolly Giant Commons were discovered slathered with shaving cream and feminine hygiene products. All the vehicles appeared to be associated with fun-loving fraternities well known for nocturnal, prank-enriched cultural activities.

· July 5, 1998 12:14 - 1:17 a.m.
As party pals hooted and whooped
Police were brought into the loop
They found celebrations
at several locations
And the parties, once hearty, were pooped.

· August 27, 1999 9:37 p.m. Same deal.

9:48 p.m. More of the modulations.

10:30 p.m. Hello, police?

10:40 p.m. I'd like to report a party.

10:47 p.m. A really loud one.

11:18 p.m. No, really loud.

11:52 p.m. Look, I know the adjective "really" is overused, but... You will? When?

· August 28, 1999 12:23 a.m. Great, can you tell them to hurry?

12:24 a.m. Hey, how's it going, fellas? Can I talk to whoever's in charge?

12:36 a.m. Hello, sir. Say, we received a complaint...

12:47 a.m. ...Because I'll have to come back if you don't, understand?

12:49 a.m. So this is just a warning notice.

· May 8, 2000 11:14 p.m. When your frisbee flies up on to the roof of a speedy laundromat, and you're young, sinewy and indestructible, you clamber up and get the damn thing.

· March 17, 2001 12:16 a.m. A college lad probably won't be phoning the units about his ticket for peeing on the Plaza.

It's actually the Judo Hut, a small City of Arcata facility for TV production and gymnastics, but for reasons unknown, the J and H have withered away, leaving us the Udo Ut.

Photo by Terrence McNally

Strange but true

• **April 5, 1994 5:10 p.m.** A man armed with a rifle near Eighth and G streets was reportedly asking people if they knew a good place to "snipe." An officer located an Arcata man who said he had been getting ammunition for the rifle and made a comment in jest that might have been taken seriously. The comic commando was admonished and released.

April 24, 1994 A resident in the 900 block of 14th Street reported a mixture of eggs, toilet paper and grass clippings thrown on her vehicle by unknown suspects just before noon.

July 14, 1994 A man asked that police document an incident involving neighborhood youth pouring ketchup on his vehicle while parked behind a shopping center in the 5000 block of Valley West Boulevard about 4 p.m.

• **August 4, 1994 6:30 a.m.** A Bayside Road man observed a male traveler attacking some type of white cloth behind his house. Officers contacted the intruder, who said he had been bathing in the creek and was trying to remove leeches stuck to his body. He was cited on outstanding warrants alleging petty theft and waste dumping with several failures to appear.

• **September 2, 1994 Morning** A man was reported pushing a baby stroller with a rocking chair on Valley West Boulevard.

• **October 15, 1994 10:15 a.m.** A man swinging a machete around in the intersection of Spear Avenue and Alliance Road attracted police interest. The suburban swordsman was evaluated and counseled, and agreed to leave the area and cease similar activity.

• **November 10, 1994 9:40 p.m.** A woman in a Siemens Hall supply closet reported hearing a man talking in a loud, firm voice on the phone, saying "Listen buddy, if you do it, I'll kill her." She then heard heavy footsteps going up and down the hallway. Police checked the area, finding nothing suspicious.

• **November 17, 1994 9:05 a.m.** A man was reported screaming at passersby in the 800 block of 10th Street. Police found the man, who said he was just excited because of his recent release from a mental health facility. He had quieted down, so the officer let him be. Two hours later and two blocks away, the man was arrested on suspicion of shoplifting at a nearby pharmacy.

• **November 30, 1994** A concerned citizen called reporting two partially nude people lolling about the Community Garden at 11th and F streets. An officer had a word with the naturalists, who agreed to move on.

• **December 18, 1994 6:55 p.m.** A Plaza social club reported a man outside throwing a radio against a wall. He told police he was upset with the manufacturer of the radio.

• **February 14, 1995** Six signs reading "If you love somebody, set them on fire" were removed from the forestry building on Valentine's Day.

• **February 18, 1995 9:55 p.m.** A report came in of someone using some type of torch in the 100 block of H Street. A Union Street resident was demonstrating fire eating techniques for friends.

• **February 21, 1995 4:30 p.m.** An Airstream Avenue resident complained of cement dust falling on his property, then turning to cement and hardening when coming in contact with dew. The concrete-coated complainant was referred to Community Services.

• **February 27, 1995 4:45 p.m.** A bundle of newspapers was reported stolen from a paperboy's doorstep in the 300 block of G Street. On March 1 at 2:20 p.m., the papers were discovered taped to the windows on the outside of the house to block the view. The perpetrator was located down a nearby alley, and apologized to the victim.

• **April 16, 1995 5:30 p.m.** A concerned citizen reported a group of people naked from the waist down throwing bottles in the area of Seventh and Union streets. A witness to the incident described them as four college-age males who had the eastbound lane of Bayside Road at Union Street blocked off with an orange traffic control cone, and that they were "dancing and mooning" at passing cars. Two of the four approached the witness' car, and he sped away, fearing that they might have urinated on it. Police found the four at an address in the 100 block of Bayside Road and admonished them regarding the behavior.

• **May 28, 1995 5:30 a.m.** California Highway Patrol officials called APD after one of their people caught a glimpse of a near-Hitchcockian tableau in the area near northbound U.S. Highway 101 by the Bayside Cutoff. A woman at the wheel of a car with its trunk lid open was said to be backing away from a shadowy figure on foot. Whatever it was all about, the scenario had played itself out, with no one in the area when a officer arrived.

2:45 p.m. A concerned Heather Lane resident described an older man sitting out front in a red car for hours, reading a book and occasionally looking up and gazing around. "I spent the morning sipping coffee and looking at this guy out the window," said the reporting party. "My cable was cut off, so it was like watching the 'old man in a car' channel." Police determined that the man was a private investigator performing surveillance related to possible insurance fraud.

• **May 28, 1995 8:53 a.m.** A traveler was described as standing at an ATM near the entrance of an I Street cooperative supermarket for "a long time," randomly punching in numbers and apparently hoping for the best. The man was warned against tampering with the machine.

• **May 29, 1995 Noon** In the throes of a hissyfit, the person outside the thrift store at 11th and K streets took it out on a refrigerator, kicking it over into the street. The icebox insulter then fled on bicycle before police arrived.

• **June 12, 1999 2:01 a.m.** Motorcycles revving in the 1000 block of Eighth Street spurred a call from an angry resident. "It was infuriating. I wanted to sleep," said the reporting party. "I gave them five or 10 minutes to shut off or leave, and when they didn't, I called APD." Police found two motorcyclists involved in warm-up procedures mere feet from the sleeping chambers of townsfolk in the early Monday morning hours.

• **June 15, 1995 1:25 p.m.** Police received a report of a "man down" on the eastbound onramp to State Route 299 at Blue Lake Boulevard. Officer Gene Pendergraft found the roadside recumbent at the ramp. "He looked dead," said Pendergraft. "I went up and shook him several times, and he finally said 'What?'" The man related a tale of hitchhiking from Arizona and getting a ride with two men headed to Yreka. Actually, they had said Eureka, and the man found himself stranded in outlying Blue Lake. He was told to give some sign of life so as not to frighten passing drivers.

• **June 27, 1995 3:02 a.m.** It started with a bang. Then a shadow passed across a woman's window. Police soon arrived, but by then, there was no one around. Case closed.

• **July 8, 1995 9:15 p.m.** A beleaguered pizza delivery guy was the subject of taunt and catcalls at an apartment building, but when police got there, everybody denied everything.

• **July 9, 1995 6:15 a.m.** A man who pumped $20 worth of gas at an Alliance Road mini-mart about 3:30 a.m. and then announced he had no wallet promised to return. After a couple of hours with the pumper pauper a no-show, mini-mart officials phoned police. Case pending.

• **August 26, 1995 11:25 p.m.** A security guard reported someone hiding in the bushes near a Sunny Brae dentist's office. Police found another security guard watching the first one as part of his training.

• **September 23, 1995 10:50 p.m.** A woman complained of a neighbor putting cigarette butts on her car due to problems between the two. By the time police arrived, the woman had put the butts on the suspect's car. The officer suggested she remove them and call in again if there were further problems.

• **September 26, 1995 12:38 a.m.** The U.S. and earth flags were discovered stolen from the Plaza flagpole. Unknown suspects cut the steel cable securing the banners. The flags are currently being replaced, and the flagpole is being modified to prevent a recurrence. This is the second theft of flags from the Plaza pole. Two years ago the Stars and Stripes was returned to the *Union* after a theft by an anti-Nixon activist.

• **October 26, 1995 8:09 p.m.** A man was seen hitting and beating on his car at a Union Street residential inn. The vehicular hissyfit was over when police got there.

• **December 23, 1995 11:15 a.m.** The figure stood alone, slumped against the stark pastel wall of the downtown bookstore. Morning shadows crept and grew shallow, but the figure remained unmoved until an employee could wait no longer. Out the door, onto the sidewalk, close enough to speak, and to hear.

The approach was articulated, but hung near, stalled in the morning air as no movement, no response stirred the stolid subject of the entreaties. Was it a choice, a statement? Or a condition, even an emergency?

Sirens, crackling radio chatter, white linen. Doors swing open with purpose. Horizontal blue and red sifting in though the bookstore stacks. A roaring of engines, wailing siren screams Doppler-shift as they fade toward the emergency room.

Case closed.

• **January 5, 1996 7:14 p.m.** A too-tall cab-over camper collided with an awning adorning the drive-thru lane at a Valley West burger palace, shearing it and a light fixture from the wall. As the brilliant orange overhang and its crunched truss lay akimbo across the vehicle, the driver ordered two double cheeseburgers, onion rings and a pair of Cokes at the window. "He got his burgers," said a highly-placed employee on condition of anonymity. "He enjoyed them, too."

With the drive-thru operation paralyzed and in crisis, the traveler from Red Bluff reportedly scarfed the bag, looking on as an employee with a crescent wrench toiled to disengage the wreckage. That done, the driver pulled back around to the back of the restaurant and parked, emerging from the cab to declare that he was not at fault and wouldn't pay, even though the awning's 14 1/2-foot clearance is clearly posted. The employee estimated the vehicle's height at an easy 16 feet.

Eager to put the run-in with the Red Bluffian behind it, the business chose to absorb the cost and soldier on in the burger wars. Repairs estimated in the low three figures will be completed this week, said the employee.

• **January 16, 1996 2:58 p.m.** As an employee at a downtown store glanced at a man who was leaving the business, the man picked up a large backpack which had been resting near the door and flashed what the employee described as "the traditional obscene gesture."

"That's a little far-fetched," thought the employee, who walked around the counter to quiz the flippant fellow about the gesture.

"You think that I stole something, don't you?" the patron, a 20-something man, said while shouldering his pack in the store's doorway. "It didn't occur to me that you stole something," responded the employee, who then instructed a colleague to summon police, and told the hostile patron, "You are under citizen's arrest."

The customer fled, with the employee in pursuit. Around the corner and a couple of blocks away, the employee's quirky quarry cut through a yard and disappeared.

"The guy was one of those flipped-out ones," said the employee, who admitted to being taken aback by the "pretty abnormal, off-the-wall" gesture. "Wouldn't you be?" he asked. "I think he had a bad conscience and probably did steal something."

• **March 13, 1996 2:39 a.m.** A Union Street man awoke to a knock at his door, but no one was there, so he went back to sleep. Ten minutes later, another knock bestirred the resident, who opened the door to see "some drunk" standing outside. The man said he was looking for someone and gave a name, but his speech was slurred and the name was unintelligible. When the resident asked for clarification of the caller's intentions, the apparently mixed-up fellow said, "Uh, uh, uh..." and ran away. The sleepy resident notified police and went back to bed. Officers found no one in the area.

• **May 27, 1996 8:28 a.m.** A thief with apparent special needs made off with close to 400 rolls of toilet paper and a couple of cases of disposable diapers from an Alliance Road supermarket. The merchandise was on pallets on the store's back loading dock when the toilet tissue taker struck, wiping out about one-third of the store's delivery of Western Family brand bathroom tissue. The loss was valued at around $100. No suspects.

• **June 2, 1996 10:54 p.m.** The fellow driving along on sidewalks at an apartment complex turned out to be a late-night fish tank deliveryman; no problem.

• **June 14, 1996 7:57 a.m.** Eviction made strange streetfellows in the 500 block of 12th Street when a couch was left in the roadway as a resident moved out in a big hurry. The foundling furniture was deemed no menace to passersby.

• **June 17, 1996 12:21 - 2:09 a.m.** Officers dealt with various things that go crunch, bang and babble in the night. After breaking glass was heard at Eighth and N streets, police found two chaps who had been hitting rocks with a bat. No damage was observed. Possible prowlers were heard blundering around in front of a salvage yard on South G Street, but police found only silent desolation. In Westwood Court, a resident's patience buckled during the loud conversation of an Oaklander and his buddy outside, until the friend left.

• **June 21, 1996 1:46 a.m.** As the wee-hour crowd dwindled at a Plaza tavern, a departing patron emerged from the billiards room with a bulletin for the barmaid. "You know, you've got problems back there," said the customer. A "transient-looking" man, actually a visiting New Yorker, was said to be treating fellow pool enthusiasts to a show of Big Apple sophistication by hurling his emptied beer glasses in a trash can and urinating on top of the broken glass.

The investigating bartender bristled at the sight of about eight glasses worth of glistening shards in the garbage can, and promptly gave the impulsive urbanite the verbal heave-ho. "You're done," said the steamed employee. "You're outta here."

"No, I'm playing pool," the New Yorker reportedly retorted, grabbing a pint of beer and guzzling it. He then flung the glass into the can "just like a paper cup," according to the beleaguered barmaid, where it shattered like all the rest. She then seized the man's backpack and called police. She said the following conversation ensued:

"Hey, gimme my backpack."

"No."

"Gimme my backpack!"

"No."

"I'm going to Eureka!"

"I'll bet you are."

With the arrival of police, the prophesied visit to the I-Found-It town came to pass as the carousing cosmopolite was subsequently offered free, mandatory lodging in County Jail on a vandalism charge. Losses were pegged at $8.

"I think he flunked the course in charm school," speculated the weary employee.

• **June 24, 1996 12:42 a.m.** Two traveling men set up camp under an awning behind a City building on Alliance Road and had just slipped into their sleeping bags when they were jolted to attention by the brilliant beams of police spotlights.

"It was raining," explained one of the men. "We thought we could get out of the rain. We barely got in when the cops swept in and hit us with the lights." The two were confounded at the swift arrival of police at their illegal campsite, but said the officer would reveal no clue to his uncanny prescience.

One of the campers was naked, which prompted additional unwanted police attention. The fellow who had unclothed explained that he has to remove his pants in order to detach a prosthetic leg which is impossible to sleep with. "It's a foreign entity," he said. "For the leg to come off, the pants have to come off." The man said the right leg was severed in a 1978 bicycle accident.

The other fellow lied about the color of his eyes as the officer wrote out a camping citation in the darkness, but soon suffered a stab of remorse at the falsehood and confessed that his eyes aren't blue at all.

Ejected from the awning area, the two men said they then moved on to another weather-protected sleeping spot under the freeway overpass at Samoa Boulevard and U.S. Highway 101. "We went under the bridge where all the spiders live," said one of the men.

• **June 26, 1996 3:27 p.m.** Walk-by vandals twisted up windshield wipers and antennae on vehicles at Sixth and G streets. A victim attributed the damage to "random drunks." The victim expressed surprise that such a thing could happen in Arcata.

• **June 30, 1996 11:08 p.m.** A neighbor noticed a man in dark clothing pressed against a wall outside the window of a Ross Street residence where two college women live. "I looked at him and I made it obvious, like 'I'm checking you out, buddy,'" the neighbor said. Seeing that he was being observed, the man stumbled toward a telephone pole, which he pretended to steady himself against as he belched demonstratively. "He was feigning being drunk," the neighbor guessed, in an effort to deemphasize the peeping tom antics or seem less menacing.

The ninja nitwit then wandered off toward Sunset Avenue and wasn't found by police. An hour or so later, the neighbor's wife went over and woke up the roommates, explained what had happened and advised them to trim their shrubbery.

"We try and look out for our nice neighbors, even the ones who aren't so nice," said the man who spotted the lurker.

• September 2, 1996 10:54 a.m.

Down 10th Street an officer came
And noticed a washcloth aflame
No source was espied
But with water applied
The linen inferno was tamed.

• September 4 ,1996 3:38 p.m.
A McKinleyville man ambled into a north Arcata diner, where he applied for a job, had a bite to eat, then locked himself into a bathroom and started talking to himself. "I have no idea what his problem was," said an employee. "He was very sketchy, to say the least." Police engineered a restroom extraction and the fellow went on his way. "It was quite strange," said the worker. Employment prospects were considered dim.

• April 2, 1999 2:39 p.m.
A downtown business owner waited to use the occupied bathroom serving the Plaza level of her building. And waited... and waited... and pounded on the door. Something was going on in there. After a half-hour or so, a scruffy man emerged and confronted the exasperated businesswoman. The longtime toilet occupant registered resentment at the infringement of his bathroom solace. "I was taking a fucking dump!" he reasoned. Then after announcing that he was the president, he dashed away down the building's stairs. Left behind in the bathroom was a scorched spoon, likely used for cooking up some injectable drugs.

• July 11, 1999 7:30 p.m.
A Heroin Heights resident asked an officer to talk to his roommate about that smell. The contact was made, but nothing criminal was noted.

• August 29, 1999 5:56 p.m.
As if anyone would want to buy these particular thrift store "donations." A 10th Street would-be philanthropist was cited for littering.

• **October 9, 1999 6:39 p.m.** Two men amused themselves by throwing rocks at the high school scoreboard from a nearby cemetery. They were warned.

• **October 14, 1999 1 a.m.** A traveling man named Anawa Wacaba reported that someone unknown was trying to steal his name. Uh, call a lawyer, advised police.

• **January 23, 2000 11:56 a.m.** A large plastic pumpkin filled with an unknown substance appeared on a man's property. Police took it away.

• **February 5, 2000 9:41 a.m.** Two pieces of World War II ammunition were retrieved from a Davis Way home and destroyed.

• **February 20, 2000 10:46 a.m.** A traveling man thought he had a new best friend, until it all went so very wrong. He phoned in a report saying he had been "riding around Arcata," apparently aimlessly, in a stranger's truck when, in the 700 block of K Street, the guy pointed a gun at him and drove away with all his stuff. The victim apparently had pressing engagements, and didn't wait for police to arrive. There was no sign of him or the bad guy.

• **March 17, 2000 10:55 a.m.** A fire hydrant reached out and bit a passing City bus on F Street (or so claimed the driver), leading to a warm, witty, wacky, whimsical and somewhat poorly received story in a local newspaper.

• **March 23, 2000 10:58 a.m.** A traveling man planted himself in the middle of a Westwood Center parking lot, wrapped jumper cables around his neck and started wailing to the skies. Apparently, despite his bellowing entreaties and unquestionable personal charisma, no one wanted to associate their surplus electrons with his crappy vehicle. He left at police request.

• **May 10, 2000 6:24 p.m.** A laundry room weirdo infestation was swiftly abated.

• **May 28, 2000 11:09 a.m.** Tucked between the grimy dish

drainers and defunct Nintendo claptrap at a Poplar Drive yard sale were lethal weapons – fully functional firearms. The entrepreneur was warned.

• **May 31, 2000 5:37 p.m.** A "clean-cut" man from Phillipsville positioned himself at 14th and H streets and, apparently on a mission of some kind, disrobed down to his bluish-green boxers and tennis shoes. He then alternated between waving his garments at passing cars, fondling his private zones, playing dead and speaking in tongues. When police arrived, the man appeared disinclined toward incarceration, but was taken into custody nonetheless. The volatile vaudevillian was charged with being under the influence of a controlled substance and taken to the Pink House. "He was really on the strange side, even for Arcata," said a witness.

• **June 29, 2000 5:88 p.m.** Imagine the creep-out factor: A resident of the 1600 block of 11th Street went out to her car and found the door opened and the inside rummaged through. What scaly, wraithlike hands had passed over her stuff?

• **July 25, 2000 10:44 a.m.** An H Street resident's shrubbery was assaulted by forces unknown for reasons unknown. Whatever the compulsion, the bush batterers seem to have been desperately intent on uglifying the resident's yard.

• **November 12, 2000 7:38 p.m.** An employee of a cooperative I Street supermarket stepped out behind the store on break, lit up a smoke and relaxed, or tried to, little knowing that two alleged felonies were about to occur. As he stood puffing, two men approached, one of them asking him for a cigarette. "I said, 'No, but I'll give you the shorts of this one when I'm done,'" the employee recalled. The effort at compromise was declined, with the passerby becoming more insistent, according to the employee.

"He said, 'I really would like half of that cigarette.' I told him, 'Well, it's my cigarette.' I was on break, trying to relax. He said, 'I've never had a bad idea in my life,' and reached around his back and he was jingling something metal behind him. I said, 'Hey, man, are you threatening me?' He said, 'No, but I think you should give me that cigarette right now,' and took a step closer."

The aggressor's colleague attempted to de-escalate the confrontation, grabbing the cigarette commando and pleading, "No, don't!" But to no avail, said the employee. "He [the alleged aggressor] pushed his friend off and swung a chain with two padlocks on it at me. I dodged it, and it passed about a foot in front of my head. It woulda hit me." His breaktime serenity irrevocably shattered, the employee threw the object of the stranger's perfervid desire – a half-smoked American Spirit – on the ground, then went back inside the store and phoned police.

The suspect, a traveler, was arrested a block away on charges of misdemeanor assault and providing false information to a police officer. Those charges have since been upped to felony assault with a deadly weapon and attempted robbery.

• **November 14, 2000 10:11 p.m.** Picture this ghastly visage appearing in a backyard-facing window of your house: a leering white teenage face in misfit-thick glasses and a white hat. The peeper scampered.

• **November 26, 2000 3:33 a.m.** A guy and a girlfriend walked right into an upper H Street guy's apartment just like old friends, but as it happened, the resident had no idea who the hell they were.

• **December 17, 2000 1:02 p.m.** How long can a putative business patron hang around in a downtown shop "just looking" before he creeps out the staff? This feller was determined to find out.

• **January 7, 2001 6:35 p.m.** A traveler at Seventh and J was frustrated, and who could blame him? His battery was dead, and despite his desperate flagdown gestures, no helpful stranger was inclined to stop and give his ailing hunk of iron a needed jumpstart. After a time, he resorted to slugging and slapping at passing cars with his bare hand, though this strategy too proved fruitless, as the traveler was still immobilized when an officer reached the scene. An officer admonished him.

• **January 11, 2001 6:52 p.m.** A nearby resident became uneasy when she realized that a man had been standing in the 500 block of Fifth Street, staring at a telephone pole, for over two hours. Despite its inherent fascination, the pole's enduring appeal eluded the witness, who phoned police. The man quickly explained the misunderstanding: he had been looking at the sky. For two hours.

• **February 8, 2001 1:35 a.m.** A prudent vehicle owner secured an auto with an anti-theft club across the steering wheel, cannily placing it in such a way that the horn button was depressed. Awakened upper H Street residents phoned police, who removed the device.

• **March 15, 2001 2:59 p.m.** They never did find the lovely chap spotted riding a bike with machete in hand near an elementary school on Old Arcata Road.

• **July 21, 2001 1:30–1:33 a.m.** Noise and urine flowed freely in the 600 block of 14th Street. Dispensers of both were chagrinned into submission.

1:55 a.m. A weirdo vs. shed showdown on St. Louis Road ended, as usual, in utter humiliation for the inanimate object.

We paid $6.50 each. One week shouldn't cost $4.50 genius. Plus, it's not your place to govern if we have cable or not. We pay you on time. You are the biggest pussy for thinking we'll fuck w/your shit after you disconnect us. Come knock on our door, I'll call you a pussy to your fuckin' face, asshole.

-420!

Only in Arcata

- **October 23, 1994 9:45 p.m.** Various apartment dwellers complained of a group of people singing and dancing in Westwood Court. A Fickle Hill Road resident explained to police that he and others were "shucking beans." The jubilant legume denuders agreed to settle down.

- **December 16, 1995 9:48 p.m.**
On Alliance Road, the caller said, the youths were on a tear
They'd knocked on doors and run off at the red apartments there
Further fun was found in flinging albumenal sacs
With passing traffic splattered in the late-night egg attacks
Some residents met with police arriving at the site
Reporting an apartment where the neighbors had proposed
No one inside, if they were there, came to the door.
Case closed.

· June 20, 1996 1:56 a.m.
As closing time purged Plaza pubs
Late patrons caroused outside clubs
Hotel guests heard voices
Police traced the noises
And quelled all outstanding hubbubs.

· July 12, 1998 2:23 a.m.
Mailboxes died
Up on California Street
Whamsmacked by vandals.

· April 23, 1999 11:13 p.m. A Wyatt Lane residence was egged by forces unknown. Alexander Solzhenitsin was not seen in the area, so that rules him out.

· July 29, 1999 10:11 p.m. Dead-eyed animal heads lining the walls of a traditionalist Plaza social establishment gazed uncomprehendingly down on skateboard-bearing youths, who ran in and out of the place for jejune jollity purposes.

· August 26, 1999 7:58 p.m.
A Ninth and H noise complaint matter
Was skateboarders' sweet pitter-patter
The sound of their boards
Drives folks from their gourds
With endless fall down/get up clatter.

· October 31, 1999 9:47 - 11:12 p.m. Pumpkins died so that others might have mischievous joy.

· December 29, 1999 12:43 a.m. Nocturnal hijinx on Antoine Avenue had to do with two cars – get this – *covered with toilet paper!* Whatever might these madcap funsters think of next?

· February 1, 2000 11:29 p.m. A South H Street man complained of someone jumping up and looking in his window. Two suspects were located; one admitted the leap and peep maneuver, saying he was playing a prank on a friend he thought still lived there.

- **April 15, 2000 5:49 a.m.** Five youths were found atop a Sunny Brae middle school. They were released to very disappointed parents, young man.

- **March 1, 2000 9:41 p.m.** Children squealed with glee as they played in an Alliance Road apartment. Someone thought this a police matter.

- **June 7, 2000 11:49 a.m.** A group of schoolchildren gathered near the Redwood Lodge, and darn if somehow 911 didn't get called on the pay phone. Police soon arrived. According to a witness, when officers asked who did it, two dozen little index fingers pointed at one hangdog lad, who stepped forward with the weight of the world on his shoulders. He was admonished and will never, ever do that again.

- **November 6, 2000 1:58 p.m.** Ninth and H pals got in a bit of exercise, kicking a big ol' green ball around and bonking vehicles and passersby with it. Ben the traveler was contacted, then took his ball and went homeless.

- **November 20, 2000 10:40 a.m.**
Picture yourself on a bike in the skate park
With hand-molded bowls and ramps to the sky
Somebody narks you, you exit quite quickly
You're gone when the cops make it by.

- **March 23, 2001 11:56 p.m.** Millions of years of evolution notwithstanding, today's youth who perhaps found the rock-hurling project down the street too challenging next resorted to running back and forth on Acheson Way with sticks. Four fledgling barbarians were warned about curfew and sent home in the company of an adult.

- **March 24, 2001 6:15 p.m.** Back to stone-age recreation for a playful pair of youngsters found pushing rocks off the embankment at Samoa Boulevard and Union Street. As fate would have it, it was Officer Stonebarger who discouraged the rocky recreation.

Passive panhandling, above. Right, one of the town square's no-no signs, redecorated with dog output.

Above photo by Kevin L. Hoover; right photo by Terrence McNally

Streets

• **March 2, 1994 10:08 a.m.** An officer Saturday observed a traveling man performing maintenance on an abandoned bus he did not own in the 200 block of E Street. The man was advised to cease his altruistic activities.

• **September 22, 1994 5:05 p.m.** A woman complained of someone putting "an extensive amount" of water in her tailpipe.

• **November 22, 1994 3:45 p.m.** A Klamath man lent his truck to a stranger and called in three days later to report that the guy never brought it back. He didn't know the man's name.

• **November 28, 1994 7:20 a.m.** An officer saw a vehicle on Crescent Way with the door open and belongings which appeared to have been rummaged through. The owner said she didn't think anyone had been in the vehicle, as it always looks that way.

• **February 20, 1995 7:32 p.m.** A Buttermilk Lane man called to report his car not being in the parking lot of a Sunny Brae shopping center where said he had left it at 5:30 p.m. As the officer was completing the report, the man remembered that he had taken the vehicle in for repairs.

• **May 5, 1995 11:39 p.m.** A roaring display of automotive prowess proved a short-lived triumph for a Valley East man, who got a ticket for the unsafe exhibition of speed.

• **February 5, 1996 12:40 p.m.** An old red Batvius "Starflite" moped of possible Czechoslovakian manufacture sat flimsily chained and abandoned for years by a bank of mailboxes in the stairwell of a Union Street apartment building. Encrusted stem to stern with rust and equipped with two flat tires, crumbling saddlebags and a one-cylinder engine (which the speedometer optimistically indicates could have powered the machine to velocities approaching 40 miles per hour), the bike had graced the stairwell "since the dawn of time," as one nearby apartment dweller put it. The elderly retro-chic putt-putt, adorned with a sand dollar for a time, has been a fond fixture for residents and attained a certain legend as a free-standing alfresco jet d'art in the windblown stairwell.

Finally, a complaint came in. A Community Service Officer tagged the bantam bike as abandoned, and sent a certified letter to the last known registered owner, a San Diego resident named Cescro Bateman. Should Bateman not respond within 10 days, one of several towing services used by the City on a rotational basis will haul the forsaken scooter away for storage, with a second letter fired off to the owner giving 30 more days to claim it. After that, the business may dispose of it in whatever manner they wish.

One way or another, the minimalist machine will be moving on. "It was an old friend," another resident of the building noted somberly. The mechanical viability of the kitschy little craft is not known, though its Warsaw Pact origins may not bode well for any use as practical transportation. "I cogitated taking it," admitted the resident, "but I don't want to rebuild a Czech scooter."

• **May 13, 1996 11:30 a.m.** A City-owned traffic control sign fell into the wrong hands for a brief period, serving as decor in what was described as a "party house." The incident occurred during Bebop 'N' Brew, when a barricade at the entrance to Redwood Park was stripped of its "Road Closed" sign. An official attached to the beery jazzfest had seen the large metal sign there one moment and gone the next, as Frisbee players frolicked in a nearby yard.

The next morning, he went to the front door of the house where he had seen the Frisbee players and asked a "disheveled" person at the door about the missing sign, which he immediately spotted in the living room. "They said, 'Well, uh, I don't know you're talking about,'" recalled the jazzy beerfest official. He then pointed to the sign sticking out from behind the door. "I said, 'It's that one right there.' They said, 'No we got that somewhere else.' I said, 'OK, fine.'" Next stop was the police station, where the purloined placard's position was pinpointed.

At the appearance of officers, the swiped sign was swiftly surrendered, and again it graces the Public Works department's inventory of traffic control hardware.

• **June 21, 1996 Late Report** An Ernest Way resident reported that a friend had left a street sign at his home. The sign, which was found on Janes Road near the fire station, was picked up by Public Works and now graces their collection of roadway artifacts. Apart from some marking-penned graffiti, it looked brand-new, had no mounting holes and bore a streetsweeper warning not relevant to Arcata. The sign's origins remain shrouded in mystery.

• **March 31, 1999 4:15 p.m.**
To re-attain bladdery bliss
A traveling man took a piss
At Ninth Street and K
Soon a cop came his way
And told him he shouldn't do this.

• **June 3, 1999 8:27 a.m.** On upper Beverly Drive, a pickup truck bearing a bumper sticker that reads "Earth First out of Humboldt County" rumbled up to a logging site across a message spray-painted on the road in two-foot letters, reading "Fuck you tree killers."

• **June 5, 1999 10:17 p.m.** A man complained of people following him from Eureka, and when contacted, they admitted doing so. They had thought it was a friend. What a big mixup.

• **June 15, 1999 9:17 p.m.** Let's conjecture on the quality of life of those who prioritized and used their personal time to administer damage to a laundromat banner.

• **August 20, 1999 7:06 p.m.** It's getting so a man can't even pee while walking down K Street anymore without someone calling the cops on him.

• **September 5, 1999 2:27 p.m.** Young lads with skateboards hung out on the Plaza, which just didn't sit right with one man. He was first heard from far away, "yelling and screaming and cursing about everybody and everything," said a witness. "Yaaaaaaarrrrrgh!" he was quoted as saying. The vocalist approached the wheeled teens and tried to take a skateboard, but the alert teen "jerked back." At that, the man reportedly tried to grab the youth's arm, growling, "C'mon, c'mon." The youth pushed him away, and at least one of the teens was ready to take the errant fellow on. The alleged aggressor then wandered a short distance away, perhaps mustering his will for the next ill-conceived onslaught, which involved another arm grab, again resisted. An associate of the man then walked him away. It was not long before the fellow was seen standing in the intersection of Eighth and G streets, yelling, "I'm not in the street!" An officer finally got his attention, and though the man didn't like the idea of a citizen's arrest, matters were pretty much out of his hands at that point.

• **September 10, 1999 1 a.m.** A man whizzed on an historic downtown storehouse, and with the evidence still glimmering in the moonlight, was cited.

3:04 a.m. Two of the new breakaway street signs along Seventh Street were left seriously akimbo, arguably even cattywampus, by vandals.

• **September 15, 1999 8 p.m.** A drunk became mesmerized

by his reflection as he peed on the window of a 10th Street environmental center, and fell into it, causing breakage.

• **September 16, 1999 2:11 a.m.** Willie, Mike and Myles chose an alley behind a hotel full of sleepy lodgers to have an argument as loud as it was pointless.

• **September 28, 1999 1:58 a.m.** A traveling man was arrested on a charge of playing with fire, possession of illegal fireworks and cocktail bewitchment in the 900 block of I Street.

• **October 12, 1999 Late Report** A construction worker at the new roundabout at Samoa Boulevard and Buttermilk Lane reported a reckless driver. It may have been one of the many people who just can't reconnoiter a proper passage around the thing.

• **October 13, 1999 11:09 p.m.** Back and forth on Alliance Road north of Spear Avenue rode the motorcycle, the mortar-like music of its muffler serenading everyone within a quarter-mile earshot. The oblivious offender was told of the complaint, and dully nodded his head in oxen-like fashion, dimly realizing that recalcitrance would result in a vaguely perceived form of discomfort. He went somewhere else.

• **November 2, 1999 2:15 p.m.** A high-density cluster of apparent information junkies condensed around a windowed obelisk in the 800 block of I Street. An officer's presence inspired wanderlust.

• **November 6, 1999 10:54 a.m.** Apparently, illegal nunchuck sticks somehow enhance information gathering at the I Street public notice kiosk. They aren't mine, said a traveler, so an officer took them away.

7:28 p.m. Fifth and I streets, where nothing much ever happens. Except this day, when a feller whipped it out and enjoyed short-lived bladder bliss. Then an officer arrived and started writing.

• **November 7, 1999 12:29 a.m.** A downtown donut shop was a virtual petri dish for festering interpersonal tensions, culminating in a woman busting a window. No prosecution was desired.

• **November 12, 1999 2:24 a.m.** Cowboy-hatted sodbusters in a brown Ford F-150 pickup truck wrought spinout damage to two areas of the play field at the Community Center. It is not known whether they yelled "Yeehaw" during the act.

• **New Year's Day 2000 4 p.m.** A gibbering nut job sat at the outdoor tables of a downtown coffee temple, spouting unsolicited aggro word salad at passersby. And then he was gone.

• **January 5, 2000 5:04 p.m.** There are kind, sensitive, thoughtful skateboarders (really, there are!) and then there's the boorish buffoon careening up and down H Street. Roller Lout eluded detection.

• **January 18, 2000 6:27 p.m.** Welcome to the hydrocarbon effulgence issuing from my noisy motorbike. This was the message received too loudly and clearly from a dimwit riding up and down Panorama Drive near Panorama Court. The brazen biker was gone when police arrived.

• **January 23, 2000 2:30 a.m.** A big, pointless whoop-te-do yelling match in front of an all-night supermarket on F Street.

• **February 25, 2000 1:20 a.m.** A person reported hemorrhaging the delicate ambiance of a downtown doughnut shop was asked to leave.

• **March 12, 2000 11:49 p.m.** Some guy was super-pissed off in front of the bowling alley, and police were asked to show the colors. They talked to issue-boy, and he agreed to quieten down.

• **March 13, 2000 9:53 p.m.** How's this for a job description? Wander the streets – in this case, the 1500 block of 11th Street – knock on doors and ask for money. Contacted by police, a McKinleyville man agreed to discontinue his chosen craft.

• **March 15, 2000 1:39 a.m.** Members of the non-cost effective gender again demonstrated the vast untapped comedic potential of testosterone. Seems the fun-starved lads had engaged in boyish "horseplay" in front of a Plaza sports bar. In the spirit of male bonding, one chap had reportedly been choked until unable to stand. Apparently he recovered from all the fun, as no further action was taken.

2:04 a.m. The choked-up horseplaymate was arrested on a DUI charge at 16th and G streets, his evening of frivol capped by a stay in a small concrete and steel room.

• **March 20, 2000 8:14 p.m.** A Blue Lake man was observed sitting alone in the dark in his car behind a Valley West motel while perfectly good network sitcoms went unwatched.

• **April 19, 2000 3:32 p.m.** An errant skateboarder slammed into a man near the Community Center, setting in motion a chain of events which will likely end in skaters being banned from the area around the center's entrance. Again, as in so many facets of public life, a singular moron ruins things for everyone.

• **April 20, 2000 2:28 p.m.** Meanwhile, downtown, a man perhaps absorbed in thought over String Theory and its potential as a unified theory of physics was warned about casually taking a whiz right there in the 800 block of G Street.

• **April 22, 2000 1:53 - 2:02 a.m.** A Manila man drew attention to himself in the alley behind Tavern Row by going potty in public, then was arrested on charges of public intoxication and marijuana possession and lodged in that ghastly multi-hued jail which dominates the county seat.

• **April 24, 2000 12:03 a.m.** Unknown adhesive enthusiasts strung duct tape across the intersection of Samoa Boulevard and H Street. An officer removed it.

12:07 a.m. This time, clear packing tape was strung across 11th and H streets. Again, an officer undid the mischief.

9:48 p.m. You have to wonder what was going on in the guy's life for him to slam his car door in the 700 block of K Street so hard the window shattered.

• **May 24, 2000 8:31 p.m.** A fellow with anger-management issues emitted loud, consonant-rich noises from a writhing hole located between his nose and chin, all because a customer lingered in the doorway of a midtown pizza take-out just a little too long, blocking his entry for a couple of seconds.

• **May 27, 2000 12:24 a.m.** A motorcyclist lost it in the roundabout at Samoa Boulevard and Union Street. He got up, dusted himself off, gathered up the remnants of his dignity and drove away.

• **June 20, 2000 7:33 p.m.** At least the nightmare of denial and the sphincter-clenching fear of all cop cars is over. A Eureka man was cited and released for driving with a suspended license; false evidence of registration; expired registration; and no proof of insurance. Wouldn't it simply have been easier just to do things right and proper there, bud?

• **June 30, 2000 4:43 p.m.** Another one of those bouquets of driving/vehicle offenses that bespeak irresponsibility and denial: drunk driving, suspended license and no proof of insurance. Oh, and jail.

• **July 19, 2000 11:48 a.m.** A traveling man found himself in a challenging predicament: He was literally an entire block – a minute's walk – from the public restroom, and yet he had to go. The age of instant gratification having permeated his nether regions, he just went in the alley behind the 800 block of G Street. After being cited, he then enjoyed a second sense of release in as many moments.

• **July 24, 2000 2:29 p.m.** Are quarks truly the fundamental building block of matter? Has anyone ever said "Arcata Bottom" without feeling self conscious? Did Tim really need that syringe at 12th and F streets? At least regarding the last question, police thought not. They took the spike away from him and transferred him from the streets of Arcata to a very weird Pink building in the county seat. Other questions remain unresolved.

- **August 24, 2000 3:12 p.m.** Carbon-based units casually flattened ass-level foliage in front of a downtown hardware store.

- **August 26, 2000 2:06 a.m.** Maybe it was the shrubbery assaulters, who moved on to establish dominion over more challenging inanimate objects. In any case, the stop sign at 11th and H proved no match for the conquering zeroes. Public Works was to fix it.

- **September 7, 2000 12:26 a.m.** Welcome to my defective muffler, said the man in the parking lot of a high-density residential inn on Union Street, in so many rpms. He seemed receptive to a request that he move the noisemobile away from people's bedroom windows.

- **September 8, 2000 10:26 p.m.** Someone made a calculated gamble about parking in a No Parking zone on East 15th Street, and lost. Welcome to real life.

- **September 9, 2000 1:18 a.m.** The bushes at Seventh and G streets proved to be one of life's nexus points for a man of unknown address, left there by a friend who had gone to find a taxi. Imagine that your near-term well-being hinged on the efficacy of such an arrangement. But as it happens, friend and cab actually appeared and whisked the shrub-huddler to a motel room offering incalculably greater comfort and dignity.

- **September 10, 2000 1:15 p.m.** Motorcycles sonically pillaged Bayside Road, inexplicably stimulating electrical activity in helmet-clad pleasure center neuroreceptors.

- **September 29, 2000 12:46 p.m.** One person's character deficit became another's repair bill as an unknown person of challenged driving skills interfaced with a Bayside Road fence at some speed. The culprit's limbic system basically took over at this point, overruling the outer cortex and dictating flight from the scene.

• **October 5, 2000 12:58 a.m.** Some locals just had to gain access to a little Eighth Street head shop, and chose the subtle method of flinging themselves at the door, as though the proprietor was puttering around inside at this hour and would be willing to open up to make that big midnight roach clip sale.

• **October 6, 2000 7:32 p.m.** A man paid for his gas at a G Street petrol mart, then went back to his car, where he was panhandled. His request for a donation declined, the importuner then made an alternative business proposal, blocking the man's entry to his car and offering to sell him some "weed." Neither proposition having engaged the driver's imagination, he instead called police, who couldn't locate the scuzzy entrepreneur.

• **November 2, 2000 8:27 a.m.** Not only were two barbarians holding forth at the top of their lungs as best their 500-word vocabularies would allow outside a residence in the 800 block of A Street, but to reaffirm the righteousness of their respective viewpoints, they repeatedly slammed doors on a mid-'80s General Motors product. The aging Camaro had chugged painfully away when police arrived.

• **November 4, 2000 4:39 p.m.** A man was reported fondling a handgun in a vehicle near Seventh and H streets. He and his main squeeze weren't found.

• **December 9, 2000 1:04 a.m.** Singing tunelessly in a guttural growl, a man of some years placed his belongings in the gutter at Sixth and H streets, took a whiz on the graffitied utility pole there, then fumbled around in leisurely, fusty-drunk fashion, appearing to genuflect to whatever deity watches over the cocktail-infested. Doddering about on the streetcorner, conducting shadowy personal rituals with exaggerated pomp while providing a running singsong narrative, the bibulant did what he could to embody the classic streetlight-swingin' drunk. The archetypal Otis then recovered his belongings with studied insouciance and gamboled shakily up the block, where police met with him briefly.

• **January 21, 2001 4:07 p.m.** Police told the fun couple they couldn't tinker with their hunka-crapmobile on a public roadway.

• **January 23, 2001 6:51 p.m.** A downtown professional enjoyed one of the perks of an Arcata worklife – being able to walk from home to office, meeting and greeting friends and familiar sights along the way. But as he neared the core of downtown, his fortunes turned as the already-narrow walkway turned into an obstacle course in front of an H Street restaurant. There, he said, two percussionists performed a drum duet, facing each other across the narrow sidewalk. As the pedestrian wended his way carefully between the bongoists, he grazed – at most, nudged – one of the musicians' hand drums. At that, the drummer became dramatist, mortally stricken that anyone would invade his space so brazenly, and rose to his feet as if to mount a physical challenge to the innocent passerby. "You mean you want to fight me over this?" asked the bongo nudger, who just walked on. Down the way, he was briefly blocked again by a bicyclist who rolled up, stopped in his path and said, "That was my friend!" Again the challenge was sidestepped, and the fellow somehow made his way to work without further incident.

• **January 25, 2001 6:25 p.m.** A woman sat on a Plaza sidewalk with an underdressed infant, begging for money. Calcutta? Lagos? Nope, Arcata. Police were called, but by then the woman had taken up her innovative parenting elsewhere.

• **February 10, 2001 4:02 p.m.** A traveler railed at the injustices of the universe with sound and fury in the 600 block of Ninth Street. He promised to calm down.

• **March 6, 2001 3:21 p.m.** Five youngsters hung out at the roundabout at Buttermilk Lane and Samoa Boulevard. An officer got them squared away.

• **March 15, 2001 3:28 p.m.** Other than the suspended driver's license, the unregistered vehicle, false registration and no proof of insurance, a McKinleyville woman at L.K. Wood Boulevard and Sunset Avenue was the ideal motorist. Cited and released.

• **March 21, 2001 3:10 p.m.** A sport-pollutility vehicle was stolen from the lot of a Union Street warren of living cubicles.

• August 17, 2001 12:46 a.m.
An artist of unknown address
Left H Street a bit of a mess
His sole decoration
A defecreation
The officer wasn't impressed.

• August 22, 2001 12:35 a.m. Maybe he thought systematically grasping each doorknob along the 1600 block of G Street would disinfect his hand, rendering it sterile and hygeinic. A traveler found there wasn't doin' nuthin', was admonished and sent on what will have to suffice for his "way."

• August 23 , 2001 12:36 a.m. An upper H Street resident may have been talking way too loud outside for that time of night, but at least he swore a lot. He agreed to take the snappy patter inside.

• August 24, 2001 6:38 p.m. A cow made a break for it on Samoa Boulevard and Crescent Way, but was easily corralled back into future burgerhood.

7:11 p.m. An H Street resident encountered a guy peeing on her flowers, and asked him to stop. He didn't, but swore at her instead. "I pull weeds there," said the resident, "and I didn't like his attitude." Though she reported his description and license plate number, the urine donor made good his escape.

• August 27, 2001 9 p.m. Ben Winker and his girlfriend walked up the alley next to the pile of burned-out rubble on Ninth Street, and there encountered a man beating a woman who appeared to be drunk in the narrow bottleneck at the alley's mouth.
"Let's go!" the man yelled, dragging the woman by the hair caveman-style. *"Fucking get up!"* he commanded his uncooperative victim while bodily jerking her to her feet. As the two passersby came astride of the neo-Neanderthal, they suggested that maybe he oughtn't be beating the woman. "Cut that out," Winker said. (As it happens, his companion is a filmmaker who recently completed a project dealing with domestic violence.)
At this, the street guy swung a roundhouse right and clocked Winker a good one, producing a classic shiner. More blows to

the head followed, and soon Winker, who is five feet, five inches tall "on a good day," was on the ground with the assailant's legs wrapped around him scissor-style, as more blows rained down on his head. "I was yelling, 'Help! Help! Police!'" he said. But none of the Ninth and H crowd, 10 to 20 of whom had assembled in a loose semicircle around the violence, offered any assistance.

Then, the woman who had been getting beaten revived herself and joined in pounding Winker, her thankless savior, and a couple of others contributed blows about the head.

Despite the barrage, Winker retained some presence of mind. "I realized that I didn't want him to go anywhere, so I started stripping him," he said, and began taking off the guy's shoes, one of which was used to batter Winker's girlfriend.

Finally, Winker and girlfriend broke away and sought succor at the liquor store at Ninth and H, where she called police. As they waited for an officer, the "urchins and drainbows" who'd been enjoying the spectacle of an innocent person being mass-attacked taunted the bloodied victim, calling him a "pussy" and suggesting that he was "hiding behind his girlfriend."

An officer arrived and asked for help in locating the suspect, but no one knew anything. Winker still thinks he did the right thing in trying to stop the abuse of the woman. "You have to live your beliefs, even when it hurts," he said.

Ben's post-gallantry winker.

• **September 2, 2001 12:54 p.m.** A Stromberg Avenue woman who'd left her car unlocked the previous night found that slithering slimewads unknown had rummaged through it. She knew this because all her stuff was dishevelled, one of her unused sanitary napkins had been stuck to the windshield and, most alarmingly, some candid photos bearing cherished memories from a recent strip poker sesh had been stolen, and may be coming to a website near you and everyone else on earth. The possibly distracted thieves did leave their sticker-slathered mini-disc player behind, and police now have it.

• **September 3 12:39 a.m.** Literally re-inventing the wheel would have been a more impressive feat than simply getting pulled over and jailed for drunk driving and being Pinked like so many others.

• **September 5 9:09 p.m.** The whole neighborhood reverse-enjoyed that arfative dog in the 1200 block of Sunset Avenue. A note was left on the front door for the owner, who wasn't home.

10:01 p.m. The *scranch* of a bottle cap being twisted off an adult beverage, the *chuff* of air rushing into the bottle, the *gloot-gloot-gloot* of liquid and bubbles trading places in the upended vessel's neck, the *snulch* of frothy goodness traveling down the galoot's gullet, the inevitable *buurrrrrrp* as carbonation wafts on wings of fetidness from the guy's face-hole – this serial symphony of sound effects preceded a second set of tedious, contrived and mercifully undocumented onomatopoeia involving an open container citation scribbled at Ninth and H streets.

• **September 18, 2001 11:41 a.m.** That guy on Bayside Road seems like another in Arcata's army of harmless eccentrics, often seen staring dazedly into the morning sun and all. But when he stands astride his bike in the middle of the vehicle lane with an eerily serene smile on his face as cars back up, it's fair to wonder what planet he's from - or still on. He was out of harm's way when police arrived.

• **October 5, 2001 9:07 a.m.** Supposedly, the guy with the Help Me sign at 17th and G streets yelled at a resident, "I'm gonna get you this weekend," then labeled him a "pussy" and an "alcoholic." The purported alcoholic pussy theorized that this was because he'd asked him not to trespass, and had escorted him off the property. Sign guy was counseled and asked to keep his comments to himself, and maybe his dogs.

11:37 a.m. An alert citizen reported someone trying to break into a parked vehicle in Valley West with some kind of tool. Actually, it was someone using a silver pen to write down the mileage of a vehicle which was for sale. What a wacky mixup!

2:18 p.m. Three menfolk were reported bickering over clothing on 13th Street, but arriving police found nothing like that. The person who called in the report then said his wallet had been stolen.

• **October 6, 2001 7:20 a.m.** Beelzebub erupted from the bowels of Hell when an I Street resident discovered Satanic writings on her porch and sidewalk. An officer found nothing too devilish, just scribblings.

4:34 p.m. Hardcore softball enthusiasts descended on Sunset School, taking a gate off its hinges, driving on into the schoolyard, breaking out a kegger and having their innings. They left on police request.

8:44 p.m. An oxygen-breathing dog struck by a petroleum-burning car in the 800 block of 15th Street was taken to a veterinarian.

• **October 7, 2001 1:41 p.m.** All kindsa weirdaloid stuff went down around town this afternoon, but by far the capper was the graffiti tagger known as "Quest," who staged his own little Pastels on the Plaza along H Street. Gabriel Molitor, 23, whipped out his black marking pen at Ninth and H and proceeded to scribble on trash receptacles, walls and windows along the 800 block of H Street. Ignoring protests from passersby, Molitor systematically drew his unimaginative tag ("Quest" means "tagger" in graffiti-speak) on every available surface. Police were called as he was halfway down the block, and when they arrived, he was marking his way past Jacoby's Storehouse.

An officer greeted Molitor, who ignored entreaties to desist and continued scrawling. When the officer attempted to take Molitor into custody, the tempestuous tagger tried to squirm away. "Getcher fuggin' hands off me, bro," he reasoned. But soon enough, his busy hands were cuffed and he was on his way to the Pink House on charges of vandalism and resisting arrest. According to the arresting officer, Molitor rationalized his defacement of a shoe store on grounds that "They kill animals to make shoes so they deserve it."

Of the victimized businesses, Molitor reportedly observed that "They should pay me to put my art on their buildings."

• **October 10, 2001 8:13 a.m.** Immobile and staring into space with an eerily beatific smile, that hinky feller was again unnerving passersby on Bayside Road. Police arrived, but by then he had marched to his different drummer away to parts unknown.

• **October 29, 2001 6:41 a.m.**
One had a hat, one a hood
And both were way up to no good
Four cars fell to ravage
Now were they just savage
Or lonely and misunderstood?

• **October 30, 2001 4:30 p.m.** Clever young minds in McKinleyville executed an ambitious ploy to demoralize teen rivals in Arcata. Utilizing a malleable medium with which McK'villers are closely accustomed, two truckloads of − get this − *actual manure* were symbolically placed near the front of the parking lot next to the proud Arcata High Tigers sign. Adorning the summit of the North-of-the-Mad-style sculptural works were butcher-paper condemnations penned by elite McKinleyville psy ops forces. Coupling unusual snacking advice with an acknowledgment of Arcata's traditional *joie de vivre* , the signs screamed "EAT SHIT GAY TOWN." Meanwhile, flyers commanded gullible readers to "BOW DOWN TO MACK TOWN." Two overenthusiastic students were later suspended from McKinleyville High School.

• **Halloween, 2001 8:16 p.m.**
A half-dozen near-naked dudes
Were out trick-or-treating all nude
A cop found the lads
Somewhat scantily clad
And sent them away freshly clued.

• **November 2, 2001 2 a.m.** An officer on a foot patrol heard a sound like someone kicking a street sign down, and that's just what it was. A toppled stop sign was located on L.K. Wood Boulevard.

6:28 a.m. Morning after morning, the brown Olds drove past the Valley East Boulevard between 6:45 and 7 a.m. And every morning, the driver blared the horn for an extended length of time, presumably for someone he was picking up there, as though it was some sort of laser horn that only the intended honk recipient could hear rather than the whole damn neighborhood. But this morning, a fed-up neighbor had a plan – call the cops in for a pre-emptive strike. The ambush worked, and the guy promised more discretion in his future horn activities.

• **November 2, 2001 10:01 p.m.** The pungent perfume of alcohol issued forth from a car unsteadily guided into a Valley West drive-thru lane in concentrations sufficient to penetrate the roiling grease fumes of the fast foodery and assail the nostrils of the kid in the window. The reekmobile, occupied by two guys and two gals of challenged sobriety, pulled out briefly into the parking lot, but rumbled away before police arrived.

11:52 p.m. We're havin' some fun now behind this Valley West motel, ain't we? And if you think things just can't get any better, you're wrong – it's bottle bustin' time, my backwards-capped friend!

• **November 3, 2001** A Buttermilk Lane resident heard some partygoers from next door stealing wood from his truck. He went outside; they ran off but eventually returned to admit the theft. They said they put it all back, but the victim, he wasn't so sure. Movie rights pending.

2:24 a.m. Those innocent guys on *Cops* never have a shirt on in the middle of the night, and neither did the mouth breather at the wheel of the small white car that whammed into a parked vehicle but kept going at a Union Street residential inn.

Love, immortalized on G Street.
Photo by Rebecca S. Bender

And at the Bayside Grange.
Photo by Kevin L. Hoover

Love

• **February 23, 1995 2:30 p.m.** A Laurel Drive woman complained of a neighbor leaving notes and gifts at her door as a "secret admirer." Police told the woman to tell the man to leave her alone, and recontact them if he continued to bother her.

• **July 21, 1995 11:59 p.m.** A Redwood Manor resident complained of a man and woman coming to his door and delivering a "strip telegram." The victim said he didn't know the two and hadn't given anyone his address. He further complained that the behavior was inappropriate, and asked for extra patrols. With his help, police located two men who were warned about the behavior and directed off campus. No woman was found.

• **September 22, 1995 7:11 p.m.** Nude and/or topless marchers en route to Redwood Park to celebrate the autumn equinox and a pagan wedding were escorted off campus and APD notified.

• **December 8, 1995 4:07 a.m.** As a woman and her husband finished up their breakfast of French toast and read newspapers at a Heindon Road diner, an older man in overalls and a red jacket sidled over, setting a folded-up newspaper next to them. "There's a really good article about Bosnia in here," he suggested to the woman, and left. After their meal, the woman picked up the unread newspaper, only to find that it contained what was later described in the sterile language of the official police logs as "illicit material."

"We were getting ready to go, and something went 'clunk,'" said the woman. Tumbling onto the counter from within the folds of the newspaper was a wooden plaque about eight by 10 inches in size, painstakingly inscribed with depictions of genitalia and other obscene references. Another item described by the woman as a "dirty magazine – people doin' stuff" was also enclosed within the newspaper.

The woman hoped to meet up with the items' donor one day so as to express her appreciation personally. "If I see that guy, he's gonna get hit upside the head with a baseball bat," she vowed.

• **December 14, 1995 1:26 a.m.** The man thought to have passed porn to an unsuspecting fellow patron at a Heindon Road diner turned up there again. An onlooker said that on this occasion the man leered at a woman in the business while licking his lips suggestively and patting the seat the seat next to him as if in invitation. The man's *savoir faire* successfully courted a visit by police, who questioned him about the other evening's incident. He said he "wasn't too sure what had happened that night," said a witness. He was advised of the complaint and asked to leave.

Shortly thereafter, the woman discovered her keys missing from where she had tossed them on the bar, and figured that the "put off" man, a longtime acquaintance, had probably stolen them out of what she guessed was "spite." After she left, the man returned, and people at the bar reportedly badgered him for the keys, which he said he didn't have. Meanwhile, the woman paid a locksmith $50 to break into her car and went home.

Later that night, she said, police called. They had run into the man, frisked him and recovered her keys, which were returned. The woman then left a message on the man's machine asking him for the $50 locksmith fee. She has yet to hear from him, she said.

• **May 30, 1996 8:29 p.m.** A caretaker at an abandoned lumber yard noticed two people enjoying each other's company on the roof of one of the disused dry-kiln buildings. A call was put through to the local constabulary, and a constable arrived within five minutes. The two were merely "doin' what comes naturally," said the caretaker. "As near as I could tell, they found a secluded place to sorta kinda make out," he said. When police discouraged the rooftop amours, the lovers took their leave. "I watch out for these kinds of things," said the observant caretaker.

• **July 4, 1998 7:19 p.m.** An Oregonian, his social skills bolstered by adult beverages, reverse-charmed females in the back pool room of a Plaza sports bar. Police performed a drunkectomy.

• **November 24, 1998 5:30 p.m.** A male was seen pulling a female into the public restroom at the syllabically formidable Intermodal Transit Facility. It was just some kids goofing around while they waited for the bus.

• **March 29, 1999 9:13 p.m.** A "totally blitzed" man clad only in sweat pants wandered in drenching rain from Stromberg Avenue to an Alliance Road apartment complex. There, he encountered a handsome 280-pound cab driver moonlighting as a security guard, to whom he tearfully confessed his loneliness. "Nobody loves me," he blubbered, beating his fist against his heart. "All I want to do is love somebody, and nobody loves me. You're somebody, and nobody loves me." "You're shitfaced," sympathized the guard. "Go home." Instead the man took a detour, scampering away, lying down in someone's muddy yard and continuing his self-pitying rant. The compassion fatigue guard warned the lonely guy that he was calling police, which offered the fellow a flicker of hope. "At least they'll love me," he reasoned. But the arriving officer was short on affection – in fact, he didn't even want to put the mud-sodden fellow in his car. Eventually, friends came and walked the loveless lad home.

• **August 10, 1999 9:35 p.m.** A boy-girl hissysnit ended with his limbic system short-circuiting, compelling him to storm from the car in a petulant frenzy. She circled Westwood Court, trolling for the wayward swain. A neighbor got nervous and phoned cops, who appeared while an officer chatted with the woman. The lovers then left the area.

• **August 19, 1999 9:40 p.m.** A 10th Street resident came home one dark night to an odd scene: A noisy public argument involving a man shouting loudly a distance away down the street. "I've lost my trust in you!" he bellowed, shouting personal details of their stormy relationship for all to hear. "It was romantic cussing," said the witness. "He drew quite a crowd." Police were called, and when they trained their headlights on the wailing swain he ended his monologue.

• **August 20, 1999 4:25 p.m.** An attractive brunette reported being followed and harassed by a male sort of person (what else?) on the Plaza. "Hi, I'm Nick," slurred the random romancer, leaning over and fouling her personal space with harsh gusts of burgundy breath. The woman, too nervous to respond, just walked away, but the "friggin' wino" didn't take the hint. Eventually she strayed too far from his base of operations, the Schwazz, and he retreated there to half-heartedly predate more disinterested babes.

• **April 16, 2000 7:49 p.m.** A couple times a week someone has to be asked to leave a 13th Street market place. Usually they're just aisle-wandering mutterers, but one suave shopper actually pinched a checker's ass.

• **July 15, 2000 9:15 p.m.** Young men – mating-age primates programmed for display behaviors – love to attract attention to their bad selves with things like loud motorcycles.

• **November 1, 2000 2:54 a.m.** A visitor to town wanted to spend an evening alone with her Arcata boyfriend at his place, without her canine companion witnessing the tryst. So, Kiya (they're all named Kiya) was consigned to the frigid camper shell outside whilst master and boy toy whooped it up inside. But dogs are said to have the most intense emotional lives of any domesticated animal, and the exiled pooch just knew that warmth, companionship and kitchen floor groundscores waited inside.

The lonely dog soon broke free from the camper shell, the door of which slammed closed with a loud, neighborhood-awakening clatter followed by Kiya wandering around the house, whining and yowling pitifully in the cold. At approximate 20-minute intervals, the dog's owner would bundle up and go outside to stuff the dog back in the truck, only to have it escape again and repeat the cycle. The whumps of the shell door closing after the lonely pet writhed free and subsequent anguished canine weeping, rendered rest by neighbors impossible.

After a couple hours of this, police were called, and they arrived in the middle of another pooch-stashing maneuver. "I was just taking her inside," the owner lied in the glare of the cop car headlights, but she did just that. The neighborhood went back to sleep and the dog owner and her boyfriend enjoyed their time together as best they could under the baleful, accusing glare of their four-legged friend.

9:50 a.m. Every time a Plaza-area worker passes by that guy with the dog, he asks her for spare change. "I always say 'No,' and he always says 'OK, cutie,' or 'Stay cute,' or anything referring to 'cute,'" related the woman. "I told myself that if he ever did it again, I was gonna tell him to stop saying that to me." Sure enough, this day's coin request came with the usual "cute" comment – "Can you spare any change, cutie?" "I said, 'No, I can't spare any change, and I don't appreciate being called "cutie."' As I was walking away, he said, 'Well, fine. Then you're ugly!' I turned around and looked at him, and he said, 'I was just trying to help you out.' So I went and called police. He apologized a couple days later. I told him he should think about that, because a lot of people probably don't appreciate being called 'cute.'"

• **November 19, 2000 10:34 p.m.** A country boy just wasn't going to leave a sexual titillation facility in Northtown, and he wasn't quiet about it. An officer pulled him out in time.

• **February 25, 2001 12:45 a.m.** A peeping tom prowled Hilltop Court, dressed in black and peering into teenagers' bedrooms. The ninja nitwit fled.

Minimalism

• **April 26, 1996 10:27 p.m.** A loud party on Canyon Drive was warned.

10:48 p.m. A loud party on Canyon Drive was cited.

10:50 p.m. A loud party on Canyon Drive was no more.

• **July 25, 1998 5:11 p.m.** Silly monkey.

• **October 3, 1998 8:47 p.m.** Bang!

• **October 11, 1998 2:36 a.m.** Oh... sorry. All these apartment doors look the same.

• **December 8, 1998 3:47 p.m.** No, you can't pay for a burger with food stamps. Go away.

- **December 17, 1998 2 a.m.** Bar closing time... a fist fight. Coincidence?

- **December 20, 1998 6:01 p.m.** Dude, it's over. Let go.

- **January 2, 1999 9:09 p.m.** An Alliance Road biz, a perv and a weenie flash.

- **November 13, 1999 9:37 a.m.** At this rate, pretty soon that barn isn't going to have any windows left at all.

- **February 8, 2000 4:51 a.m.** It seems that garbage trucks are noisy.

- **March 13, 2000 2:08 a.m.** OK, something funny's going on with that sign at S and Blakeslee.

7:15 p.m. A sex pervert moved to Alaska.

- **March 19, 2000 9:12 a.m.** A loserific mooch was asked to leave a 13th Street supermarket of choice.

12:58 p.m. As was another energy-sucking zero.

2:44 p.m. A bozo without portfolio was asked to depart from a tiny television studio at the Udo Ut.

- **March 21, 2000 5:38 p.m.** What exactly is there to steal at a tattoo parlor?

- **The 4th of July, 2000 3:16 p.m.** Kids aren't supposed to have booze.

3:55 p.m. Kids aren't supposed to have booze: the sequel.

4:35 p.m. McKinleyvillers aren't supposed to glug refreshing adult beverages on the Plaza.

4:58 p.m. Travelers aren't supposed to glug refreshing adult beverages on the Plaza.

7:34 - 10:40 p.m. People like 'splosions. Whaddya gonna do?

• **July 6, 2000 7:44 a.m.** This guy has really lost his way. Let's hope he can dig his way out of the mess he now has to deal with.

• **July 7, 2000 8:34 p.m.** Trouble in Kioskville.

• **July 20, 2000 8:52 a.m.** That guy that sits out front of that store was acting that way again. Mainly, he's too loud and his teeth look funny.

• **July 24, 2000 3:56 a.m.** She told him off and stormed out.

• **July 25, 2000 10:30 a.m.** Geez, the bowling alley's dead. Why keep beating up on it?

• **August 21, 2000 8:09 a.m.** Do they never learn?

• **October 4, 2000 12:46 p.m.** Don't need that guy in here.

• **October 13, 2000 4:38 p.m.** Get the hell out of here.

• **January 16, 2001 4:53 p.m.** There are more politic ways to say it, but someone wigged and went to the bin.

8:29 p.m. Sometimes landlords and tenants find they have differing interests.

• **March 22, 2001 7:53 p.m.** There's this guy standing in my doorway.

Much Ado

• **August 3, 1994 1:06 p.m.** A woman who had been screaming on the Plaza advised police that she had been "letting off steam" and needed no assistance.

• **February 22, 1995 2:35 p.m.** Responding to a report of a person fallen down in the 1400 block of G Street, an officer found a pedestrian who had "incompletely stepped off the curb" and suffered a minor injury. The victim chose to treat himself.

• **March 26, 1995 1:10 p.m.** Ten newspapers spilled from a delivery vehicle at the Blue Lake Boulevard exit from a eastbound State Route 299. To the annoyance of police, the driver had reportedly been heard later to remark that he was aware of being 10 papers short due to the spill, which he apparently made no effort to remediate. Concerned observers picked up the windblown pages. "We commend the citizens who cleaned it up," said Officer John Desadier.

• **May 29, 1995 8:56 a.m.** In bags it lay, under an nondescript bush on a busy street, unnoticed. The suspicious material piqued the woman's curiosity, and she looked closer. What she saw there that day led quickly to a call to police, for the bags' contents had once been...*alive*. Police determined that it was discarded beef jerky.

• **May 30, 1995 2:40 p.m.** You don't go after a padlock with bolt cutters in broad daylight two blocks from the center of town without attracting police interest. That's what a team of landscape employees learned when they tried to cut away a jammed lock at a work site near Sixth and H streets. No crime.

• **June 5, 1995 11:15 p.m.** From within the house of the holy shone a light that could be dimmed by no man. An annoyed neighbor complained about the blaring bulb, but several other tenants told police the light had been installed by the church and there was just no way to turn it off.

• **July 13, 1995 8:40 a.m.** A woman reported her residence having been pelted by strawberries, but no permanent structural damage was traced to the fruity impacts. Strawberries, the edible fruit of temperate herbs of the genus *Fragaria*, are enlarged pulpy receptacles bearing numerous externally mounted seeds, and form the basis of many popular summertime dessert treats.

• **October 21, 1995 5:01 p.m.** A skateboard squad on the high school quad refused to leave without a prod. Police were hailed, the kids had bailed, the case was closed when searching failed.

• **February 9, 1996 10:31 - 11:30 p.m.** A foul flurry of far-flung frenzied Friday fetes found fretting folks fussing from the feverish folly. Noise complaint warnings were then issued at parties on Cropley Way, Spear Avenue and Wisteria Way. The clueless Cropley carouser carried on cacophonous clamor causing complaints to continue; consequently, cops came and calmed the crew with a censorious citation.

• February 17, 1996 2:42 a.m.
In the air one early morning, drums provoked a noise report
Loudly pounding sounds aborning, thrumming up from Tilley Court
Police arrived, one man recalled, tempered the percussion quest
Asking "Just calm down," the ill-timed bongo fest was laid to rest.

12:36 p.m. An H Street woman reported the theft of two houseplants in an audacious heist that went down in the early morning hours of Saturday.

About 3:30 a.m., according to a roommate, a resident heard someone enter the home through an open door, then run back out. Looking out her window, she observed a man bounding down the street with two large potted plants, a China doll and a lily, one under each arm. She then sprung from bed and gave chase as the man hopped a fence into a yard on the next block.

Going around to the front door, the woman confronted the man, demanding the plants back. She said he denied fleeing with any filched foliage. When asked what he had been carrying, the man reportedly said it was bags of groceries from an all-night supermarket across town.

After the plants' owner notified police the next afternoon, officers went and had a talk with the suspect. Soon the plants were back with the owner, who declined prosecution.

• March 27, 1996 10:15 p.m.
Out behind the mall
"Weird" lights and sounds were described
Police found nothing.

• April 8, 1996 1:05 p.m.
A beleaguered G Street sandwich shop, recent survivor of graffiti, break-ins and vandalism (including the dismantling of its roof), has now been raided for the twinkling

Christmas lights adorning a small tree outside the door. Lilliputian loggers lopped the light-bearing juniper, taking it and the lights. "It was three feet, now it's like, two," said an employee. "I don't understand why."

• **June 14, 1996 2:10 - 11:09 p.m.** Perhaps future historians will better understand why the burglar alarm went off over and over at a Sunny Brae medical office. The cause is presently unknown.

• **August 25, 1997 2 p.m.** G Street neighbors had a run-in over a trellis, the foliage clinging thereto and allegations of snoopery. Resident A, fed up with what she described as the Mrs. Kravitz-like nosiness of her neighbor, erected a trellis along their mutual fence.

On A's side, jasmine has grown, offering a visual barrier against resident B, who is said to actually stand on her chair to enhance her view of the goings-on at A's place. B maintains that the trellis is in her yard, and wants it removed. But, said A, "If she wasn't peeking over the fence and being nosy, it wouldn't be there in the first place."

B denies the surveillance. "I'm not curious about her," B said. "I'm too short to see over a six-foot fence." B said that when A invaded her yard to erect the trellis, B made a joke of it, asking, "While you're at it, would you trim my rosebushes?" but received no reply. B further claims that all the bushes A has planted obstructs the view from the street and blocks sunlight from reaching B's bedroom window. "We have an upstairs window that overlooks her yard, and how she's going to cover that, I don't know."

Police reports say the two "agreed to disagree" on the matter, which both parties confirm. The trellis' fate is unclear.

• **June 10, 1998 6:50 p.m.**
A citizen called in to say
That three straying bales of hay
Had somehow been dropped
On Samoa they plopped
Cops helped get them out of the way.

· September 2, 1998 9:21 a.m.
A circular pathway was traced
By someone who, back and forth, paced
At 14th and F
But he gave up and left
When a friend never showed at the place.

· September 28, 1998 Late Report A faucet leaked at a Fifth Street religious facility.

· August 8, 1999 3:35 p.m. Citizens of Ninth and H quibbled loudly about nothingness.

· October 12, 1999 1:46 p.m. A women positioned herself in the hallway of an historic Plaza storehouse and took to orating in a histrionic fashion just this side of menacing. Waving her arms around and striking poses, she offered fragments of a semi-coherent monologue which, in sum, added up to senseless word salad. Police asked her to go away, and she did.

· January 5, 2000 2:15 a.m. An officer noticed an open panel on an Arcata Volunteer Fire Department truck. Nothing had been stolen, so perhaps the opportunistic panel opener had been interrupted in his or her inquiries. A pickaxe recently stolen from a AVFD truck has been replaced, though the original is still in the hands of a person of dubious morality.

· August 2, 2000 11 p.m. A poncho-clad man was escorted from a City Council meeting after he refused to endure opinions which did not coincide exactly with his own, and became disruptive.

· August 18, 2000 10:24 p.m. Some sort of a West Side Story street scenario withered in the glare of police car headlights in the 700 block of Sixth Street, with several participants in a fisty encounter scattering under the unexpected photon barrage. This one lady said she didn't know nothin'.

· August 26, 2000 10:49 p.m. Someone threw a bag of poop on a Maria Court porch and scampered away in triumph.

• **August 28, 2000 5:19 p.m.** A Plaza businessperson asked tobacco enthusiasts to move, but they wouldn't, so the government was brought to bear on the matter.

• **September 12, 2000 2:12 a.m.** Ocean breezes sweep the Mad River's flood plain, stirring the wind chime to life on an outer 11th Street lady's porch. Or did, till some schmuck stole it.

• **October 14, 2000 3:13 p.m.** A resident in the 500 block of 12th Street reported the theft of a small length of rope she uses as a dog leash.

• **November 16, 2000 5:58 p.m.** A Valley West motel and a fast food stand reported a special sort of guy caught in the corporate neon glow that effulges the area. After creeping out motel personnel, the rugged individualist was observed climbing a ladder onto the roof of the greasery, perhaps in search of long-vanished Golden Arches. An officer briefed the traveler on his popularity, and the news was not good.

• **December 22, 2000 1 p.m.** It falls on future criminologists reviewing the annals of 20th century crime to give historical context to an incident wherein a woman is reported to have "flipped off" a man near the bus station.

• **January 4, 2001 12:07 a.m.** After being called a "fascist" and getting sworn at, an Arcata mayor asked cops to escort idealists from City Council chambers so that she might be able express her opinion without yelled interruptions.

• **January 12, 2001 1:36 p.m.** A resident near Stewart Park complained of excessive noise, but an officer detected only routine, glee-oriented emanations.

• **February 9, 2001 7:09 a.m.** People argued in front of a Northtown gas station, assuring their place in Arcata history.

• **February 26, 2001 3:48 p.m.** A raised-voice kerfuffle at Ninth and H amounted to naught.

• **March 15, 2001 1:35 p.m.** A McCallum Circle resident was reported running a power saw "just to make noise." He agreed to quiet down, and a relative was arrested and jailed on charges of public drunkenness and probation violation.

• **March 27, 2001 1:39 p.m.** Discarded husks of computer game CDs were discovered in a bag in Safeway's newspaper recycling bin and returned to the victimized video store at Seventh and F streets. Titles included *Unreal Tournament, Supercross, Knockout Kings, Metal Gear Solid, Top Gear Daredevil, Smuggler's Run, Tekken Tag Tournament, NBA Shootout 2001, Jet Moto 3* and *NBA Shootout 2001.* The thieves may have been dishonest, but at least they were discerning.

Late Report A burnt matchbook was found by a dumpster in the 500 block of H Street.

Someone didn't like finding a plywood portrait in their yard.

Photo by Kevin L. Hoover

Thomas J. Doyle and drummer.

Photo by Terrence McNally

Appendix 1

Bad People Doing Wrong Things
Thomas J. Doyle

The neon glow of Tavern Row
Lights up a fist lubed up
On Friday night
Knuckle sandwich and cocktails
An APD delight
Across the way at Ninth and H
The sidewalk's clogged
With a clump of dreads and nugs
Sift through slang and patches
And cart away the thugs
The weekends are always this way
And needless to say mistakes are made
There's things in this town that you don't want to know about

Bad people doin' wrong things
Bad people doin' wrong things
Next stop's the House of Pink
Bad people doin' wrong things
You know
You'll never get away with it *oh*
You better try and savor it *oh*
Gotta let you know

He's got a P.O., she served him an R.O.:
He's banned from the Blue Lake Roller Rink
He peels out in his T-Bird
He's takin' it to the brink
It gets mean, pushing a 415
He's back in town, hopped up and breakin' rules
His net worth in warrants
Could put your kids through school
This goes on an' on
And he's bellowing shirtless out on the lawn
Firearms and an indoor grow,
Craning over a line as the cops come rolling up

Bad people doin' wrong things...

Appendix 2

Glossary

An Historic Plaza Storehouse – There's only one.

Big Bill – See McKinley.

Bongos – Percussion instrument of Cuban origin, frequently emplyed as trance-inducing/torture device on the Arcata Plaza.

Bonking – Bongo flagellation. Means something else in England.

Breakfast Club – They who drink from bags in a secluded Marsh hollow.

Dine 'n' dash – See scarf 'n' scram.

Dirt Merchant Central – See Ninth and H.

Djmbe, conga – Along with other hand drums, often mistaken for bongos.

Fill 'n' flee – To engorge your 12 mpg Planet Killer with dead dinosaurs from places where they hate us, then roar away without remunerating the underpaid attendant.

Fun Bunch – Travelers who meet in the railroad easement behind a mini-storage yard.

Fun Bunch World Headquarters – Trackside lair of the Fun Bunch.

Gauntlet, The – See Ninth and H.

Heroin Heights – A working class neighborhood south of Samoa Boulevard.

Hovel grovelers – See Scrounge lizards.

Intermodal Transient Facility – The Intermodal Transit Facility, created in 1994, located across from the Arcata Service Center.

I Street Cooperative Supermarket – The Arcata Co-op, store of legend and aisleway huggery.

Judo Hut – See Udo Ut.

Marsh – The Arcata Marsh and Wildlife Sanctuary.

McKinley – Twenty-fifth U.S. president, immortalized in a statue on Arcata's town square.

Mojo-harshing – A form of brutal oppression exercised by law enforcement having to do with interrupting cosmic bongo vibes.

Ninth and H streets – Also known as The Gauntlet, a streetcorner when sitarounders, hangabouts, dirt merchants, nomads and police congregate. Newly regentrified for your convenience as of 2003.

Nugs – Cannabis gemlets traded 'twixt Plazoids and beyond.

The Plaza – Arcata's multidimensional town square, home to statute of William McKinley.

Pink House – The Humboldt County Correctional Facility.

Pirate, The – L. Scott Rebman, deceased.

Ragman – Pete Villarreal, aka Rags, aka Raggedy Pete.

Redwood Park – A great meadow surrounded by redwoods. A City of Arcata production.

Scarf 'n' scram – To eat a restaurant meal and bail on the bill. See dine 'n' dash.

Schwazz – The Plaza in stoner.

Scrounge lizards – Ninth and H habituees.

Scroungeloids – See Scrounge lizards.

Thirteenth Street marketplace, A – Wildberries Marketplace, your supermarket of choice.

Udo Ut – The Judo Hut, a multi-use City of Arcata building where the J and H on the sign have freakishly withered away.

Appendix 3

Police Log Headlines

Sidewalk nug-yearners moved to minimal extertion
Short-range missiles are for lovers
Seven-princess play a 'hoot' for neighbors
Sloshed pseudo-sailor linked to tire-tape caper
Parking spot spat brings bastardly blowback
Beige leisure suit and inhabitant banished from bar
A smashing faux pas at the negligence festival
Might as well declare drunkenness the 51st state
The desperate note – an underappreciated form
So many brain cells, so little time
Fence stretchers trade sour smoke for pocket litter
Nipple vs. hash brown showdown perils meal completion
Horned blowhard offers domestic tranquility – for a price
Psiloshroomer, please put down the white courtesy phone
The meathead who mistook a customer for a 'Chronic' case
Collect call for anyone who wants to be sworn at and threatened
Yard poopers wear out neighborly welcome
Spokesnomad obfuscates
Piejacking fails; jar of toes not worth beans
Crust tossers hosed to a sitstill
Maybe those Temperance League ladies were on to something
Pleasuredomes, pottydomes pop up, prompt police patrols
Restroom requirement eludes peesome threesome
Plazafarians go riparian
Lock up your dirt
Relief is just an apology away
Ripoff rocketeer jettisons pooch to attain escape velocity
Grasp on reality considered tenuous
Gaily garbed hoi polloi clash with selves, others
With asses that bad, they might just mean it
THC Tribbles, spindled tipplers trigger trouble

Captain Tantrum and the greenshirts
Cupid's packing a BB gun these days
She weirdlings try to ruse their way into homes
A solid wall of needless, noxious nimrod imbroglios
Small-town hijinks push quaintness envelope
Looking for love in all the wrong doorways
Morning lawn wallower transcends mere pants
Nabobs, ne'er-do-wells and a missing hundred bucks
Belligerent bliss, vituperative spiritual advice
Professor Harold Hill's lost that certain zing
Cig chuggers clown for the camera
Renegade refuse-nik violates virtuous dumpster
The *North Coast Eye* – a 'stuped little paper'
Grabby extremities implicate host torso
Horizontal halitosis hobbyist repositioned
Huffin' by the old condom trough
Salty snack cascade sours sweet talk
'Tis the season to be creepy-crawly
Fleeting moments of drama punctuate entropic spiral
An ass kickin', door slammin', bottle wavin' kind of week
Nimrod machinations pose enforcement challenge
She-puker provides essence of modern times
The Chapstick Invader
Dewdrop arrangement attracts law enforcement
Rugged Individualists ensure cop job security
Tofu, Echinacea heists enter annals of Arcata crime
Camo-clad lads stymied by canny mailbox
Man bites dog – journalism profs happy at last
Hash browns hijacked, sprinkler head sundered
Cannabis achievers bungle wake & bake
The ephemeral symmetry of he-said, she-said
Squinting into the flashlight beam
Neighbors say the darndest things
Facial furniture hampers camouflage effort

When that 'not so smart' feeling strikes
There's many a dip with a cup to his lip
Brain Medicine, authorized and otherwise
Furies no mobile home could ever contain
Who's to blame when the situation degenerates?
They'll never drink from *that* water fountain again
Mouth-breathin', knuckle-draggin', time-wastin' adventure
Living life to its fullest
The shackled drunk shuffle
The evocative implications and canine emanations of scruffiness
Spent swain a strenuous slug toss
Host organism expels foreign matter
Doing our part to close America's yelling gap
Hello, 911? Send a squad car and a 12-pack
Rhododendron, flower pot repel interlopers
Waved stick curtails curiosity
It ain't like in the movies
Fuzztone fog and cocktail logic
To-do list includes senseless gibbering
Hoagie shortage terminates toilet siege
Puffy jacket posse pulls on door handle
Kissy-face scenario eludes smitten swain
Green flower savior takes hose in hand
After-sale auto annihilation averted
Cue ball death grip eventually loosened
When love comes knocking at your skull
The Man's keeping us (hic) down!
Stoned souls harvested by the Grim Ranger
Opposable thumb & forefinger filch a flank
D.A. to review kitty litter bucket battle
Tensions explode in stench-retention chamber
Me and you and a drug named Boo
Wacky misadventures, some bleeding
When realities collide

The King of the Road's secret ignominy
Sixty bucks worth of bad hair
Baggy-eyed, dateless, and no wonder
Jackassishness defies sober inquiry
An ascendancy of shirtless mouth-breathers
An eerie interplay of light and shadow
Not too nutty, fully freaky, but basically bizarre
Hangup harpies sear soul; carport mystery deepens
Feuds flare, buzzes harshed, kidneys taxed
Shiny objects, eerie serenity prove evanescent
Satan scribbles, auto god stalls, saggies take comfort
Wandering aimlessly through life and traffic
Bronze overcoat withstands onslaught of oaths and curses
Pooches howl, drinkers froth, saggies scuttle, slumpers sloth
Unsecured naughties fall into all-too-slimy hands
Quick as a wink, you're in Big Pink
Quick! Someone invent a clue bong!
Bard bears brunt of primal drone
Good thing they aren't the grammar police
Low-wattage discharges jolt and revolt
Silicon stimulus excites carbon-based wetware
Wardrobe rustlers pull three-load heist
Serial hooch gargler forgoes cost/benefit analysis
Man didn't bite dog, but that tree branch has an attitude
Free-range solipsists in hootful maelstrom
McKinley serenaded; travelers marinated; neighbors exasperated
But officer, it's not my fault – you see, I'm oblivious
A drug so wonderful it redefines Arcata culture
One more trip to the naughty human pound
Sub-genius solutions to hardscrabble exigencies
Irises, fairy dirt wrested from grasp of rum-ripping grocery pirate
Smoke and drink, clamber and howl, doink and bicker

Excitement, adventure, romance and handcuffs
reward wee-hour wanderers

Peripheral vision registers blurry red octagon
The late-night joys of stick and stone-age technology
Party favors include knuckle sandwiches, punch
Dogs and drunks, campers and kids gone astray
Nasty notes, pavement dramas, swamp encounters
Details are unclear, and that's probably just as well
Chump escapades mark fresh nadir of lameness
Love turns to embers, ashes and allegations
Mumbling mendicant slumps sullenly into sunset
If I take enough of this stuff, my problems will disappear
Back alley features diverging views by the fistful
Charged with life's exuberance, then other things
Earthly wanderings take steely detour
Spaced traveler succumbs to Earth's gravitational pull
Police Pink-plop persons posing menace to sobriety
Fussy smut-hunters shut slut hut's mutt, butt glut
Streetcorner drunk affects studied insouciance
Critters cry, caper, yap, nip, age and creep out passersby
Appearances can be depressing
Spiritual attainment leaves smoker unchained
Car door slamming affirms righteousness
Goodtimers greeted; porta-potties punished;
spiral of denial winds down; cuteness debated
Crash-test dummy trucks into hilltop house
Space travelers alight, befester, nebulate
Life's essentials, if not much of an actual life
Hugs, nugs and low-grade infections are for sharing
City provides hissyfit-squelching, illusion-dashing services
Ambient puppies stashed in aftermath of banal irony
Bozos gibber; cretins flash; drinkers gurge;
travelers slap; Pink House looms
1,001 ways to waste everyone's time
Spittle-pocked gank pit paved with flesh and flannel
Suffused with the sheer joy of life, or something
Panhandlers pester passersby during day;

schlubs stomp shrubs by night
Droning drums, dinky dramas, desultory dullardry
Darn that pesky old Arcata Municipal Code
Percussus resurgam: Plaza bongo pilots serenade the square
Bongos in bloom find mojo abruptly curtailed
Out was he wiped, and off were they ripped
Those two cruel, cruel words: closing time
All drunked up and no place to go
When moisture falls into the wrong hands
Chances are they wouldn't have done that in front of their moms
Vandals slather, campers snooze, loopy dudes infuse with booze
Did a million-moron march pass through town?
Low-effort Vaudevillians play the Pink House
Anti-nitwit legislation desperately needed
Sidewalk's siren song summons sprawlers
Taco, tenpins and coffee privileges annulled for voidoids
Popular dumpster used as garbage bank
Hirsute hepsters hopped up on Mary Jane
Bongos throb; hoboes mob; aggros blather, bleat in gobs
Japes, jests and jollity lead to lugubrious aftermath
Students devour animal parts in roadway
Naval incursion rocks wee-hour doughnut shop
Once-beloved carcass rots in the roadway
Cretinous parasite makes off with tip jar
Glug went the adult beverage, clang went the cell door
There's a time and a place, and this is neither
An amateur alchemist's pharma-pseudical admixture
Suddenly, everything went so very wrong
Plaza saxophonist gets his 15 minutes of fame
Personal problems go public, all too loudly
Alcohol, cigarettes, dope and loud, loud music
Shunka shuffles, punklings purge, dogs succumb to arfly urge
Person's leg attacks dog's jaws in Redwood Park
Defunct in the shrubbery; face down in cig butts
Creative driving – it's not just for cars any more

Hello, nice to meet you, let's take drugs
Dumpsters: go for the garbage, stay for the comfort
Deer outmatched in various car, dog run-ins
Hey Fido, how's about you and him fight?
Musical interlude, public family feud, tiny twerpitude
Growly howlers serenade neighbors, and so do barking dogs
Interpersonal tensions fester into verbal vituperation
Pumpkins splatted, shake snatched, 'coon dispatched
Various two, three and four-legged critters ramble
Weirdos wail; Earthlings roam; nuisance asked to head on home
Various humans and animals go astray in life
Semi-feral leisure specialists fuss and percuss
Culture, cosmicity, cadgers clog sidewalks
Some got away with it and some didn't
Begone from this place, o solipsistic swarm
"Yaaaaaaarrrrrgh!" reasoned the man on the Plaza
Escape from the land of unfair vacuum cleaners
Inanimate objects dealt with in stern fashion
The tawdry chronicle of brazen buffoonery
Cloggy sidewalkery; tattoo mockery; cocktail schnockery
The fusspot, the perv and the off-roading RV
Little monsters spare-candied by corner crew
Soft drugs, hard liquor and low-budget lunacy
Phones ripped; caroler curtailed; cocktails sipped; organism jailed
Bedeviled by several disheveled revelers
Hood banging; chem wackage; manly boneheadery
Alternative lifestyle expressed all over the street
Drinkery denizens stride boldly into ingnominy
Spiderville, a refuge from paintballs and lasers
Dumpage, thumpage, sluggards and dullards
Carbon-based units do the darndest things
Don't sleep here, don't spray there, don't say that
Fuss and bother, mud, paint, smoke and bongos
Bulgy-eyed, beef-glutted and brazen

Ticket books depleted at '420' park wingding
Lions and lizards and drunks, plus the odd dingbat
Splish, splash, screech, bang, toke, glug, zzzzz... huh?
Life forms slither, slurp chems, hurl chunks
It seemed like a good idea at the time
Clumpage, grumpage, slumpage and stompage
Sharing the obstreperous joys of louthood
Loose cows, looser drinkers rounded up
Leisure specialists tokey into the pokey
The ID they offered was a tissue of lies
Drinking deeply of life's intoxicating nectar, also hooch
Cocktail treatments yield steely side effects
Festering funk traced to medium-rare filth
Cocktail logic spurs pushy-pushy, shovey-shovey, yelly-yelly
Unleashed dogs and non-bongos suck energy
Tempestuous thugs, a bibulous bounder and a caterwauling cad

Allure of unguarded rent money, potting soil
precipitates moral collapse
Bongos aborning in the morning
Pits hit – tree implicated
Loud louts shout; fuzz bust buzz buds; cheeky sneak plucks bucks
Audio, aroma anomalies cause co-hab complaints
Pan-galactic cosmicity annoys bystanders

Pets, masters enjoy spiritual communion,
leave behind piles of dog crap
Booze-powered biker, bongo boinkers warned
Huddled masses and their puppies
Go away and don't ever come back
Raised voices, upturned bottles and flouncing
Life is so much better with you not around

Appendix 4
Coplog photo gallery

Top, Tavern Row in the olden days. Middle, in August, 1959. Bottom, in December, 2003.

Top photos courtesy Arcata Historical Sites Society
Bottom photo by Terrence McNally

Eureka's Pink House, officially known as the Humboldt County Correctional Facility.

Photo by Terrence McNally

The Intermodal Transient Facility.

Photo by Terrence McNally

The Fun Bunch play with role-playing cards near the train tracks and over the fence from a covered compost heap as the *Eye's* Cory Ratzlaff, left, looks in in anthropological fascination.

Photo by Kevin L. Hoover

The author (center) and the Arcata Police Department, 2002.

FROM THE PAGES OF THE ARCATA EYE

The Police Log

True Crime & More from
Arcata, California
Kevin L. Hoover
Foreword by Jim Dodge

INCLUDES "BAD PEOPLE DOING WRONG THINGS"

Share the Giggles!

Send The Police Log: True Crime & More from
Arcata, California to a friend.

$12.95 each, plus $5 shipping and handling to:
Coplog Book
The Arcata Eye
P.O. Box 451
Arcata, CA 95518
Allow a month for delivery.
California residents add 94¢ (7.25%) sales tax.

Subscribe to the Arcata Eye.

It's a real weekly newspaper!

Send $35 for a year's subscription to:
The Arcata Eye
P.O. Box 451
Arcata, CA 95518